Teacher's Guide to Mind Mapping

The:
» Research
» Theory and
» Practical Use
of Mind Mapping in
» Primary,
» Secondary,
» Tertiary and
» Business Education.

By Gideon King:
» Mind Mapping company owner
» Personal development expert
» Success strategist
» Entrepreneur
» Visionary
» Investor
» Author

ISBN 978-0-9803652-2-1

First published 2007

Contents

Chapter 1: Introduction to Mind Mapping 1
Acknowledgements 2
How To Use This Book 3
What is Mind Mapping? 5
The Different Learning Styles 8
Where does Mind Mapping come from? 9
How does it work? 10
Who uses Mind Mapping? 11
Mind Mapping Vs Concept Mapping 18

Chapter 2: Educational Applications of Mind Mapping 22
Educational Applications of Mind Mapping 23
Applications for different subjects 24
Learning Intelligences 26
The Four Resources Model 27
Productive Pedagogies and Mind Mapping 32
Teaching online, interactivity and hyperscapes 35
Problem Solving 37

Chapter 3: Pre-Classroom Uses 41
Lesson Plans 42
Course Planning 48
Handouts 50
Assignment Planning 52
Summaries and Reviews of Media 53
Presentations 54
Other Uses 57

Chapter 4: Mind Mapping in the classroom 59
Brainstorming 60
Advanced Organisers 62
Maths 64
Asynchronous Learning Networks 71
Tips for Using Mind Maps in the classroom 72
Conversation Maps 73
Living Documents 73
Taking Notes 74
Assignment Planning (by students) 75
Exam Preparation 76
Subject and Career Planning 77
Marking Mind Maps 80

Chapter 5: Constructing Mind Maps 85
How do I create a Mind Map? 86
Mind Mapping by Hand 86
Group Mind Mapping 89
Mind Mapping with Software 92
Hand-Drawn Mind Maps versus Mind Mapping Software 93
How to choose the right Mind Mapping software for you 94

Chapter 6: Professional development 99
What is Professional Development? 100
Information and Communication Technologies (ICT) 103
Career and Professional Development Planning 106
Research 107
Books and Articles 107
Attending Seminars / Workgroups 111
Professional Associations 112

Chapter 7: Practical Examples and Ideas for the Classroom 114
Creating Mind maps 116

Note Taking Exercise - Spoken 118
Note Taking Exercise - Written 119
Goal Setting Workshop 121
Creative Writing Mind Maps 123
Creating a Mind Mapped Lesson Plan 124
Creating a Mind Mapped Handout 126
Creating a Mind Mapped Assignment Sheet 128

Chapter 8: Resources 131
Common Mind Mapping Terms 132
About the Author 135
Mind Mapping Online Resources 140
Mind Mapping Freeware 142
Exclusive Book Owner's Forum and Extra Resources 144
Epilogue 145

Chapter 1: Introduction to Mind Mapping

This chapter introduces you to the contents of the book and explains what Mind Mapping is, where it came from and how it works. We discuss different learning styles and how Mind Mapping benefits people with different predominant learning styles. We then look at some of the many uses of Mind Mapping, as well as the differences between Mind Mapping and Concept Mapping.

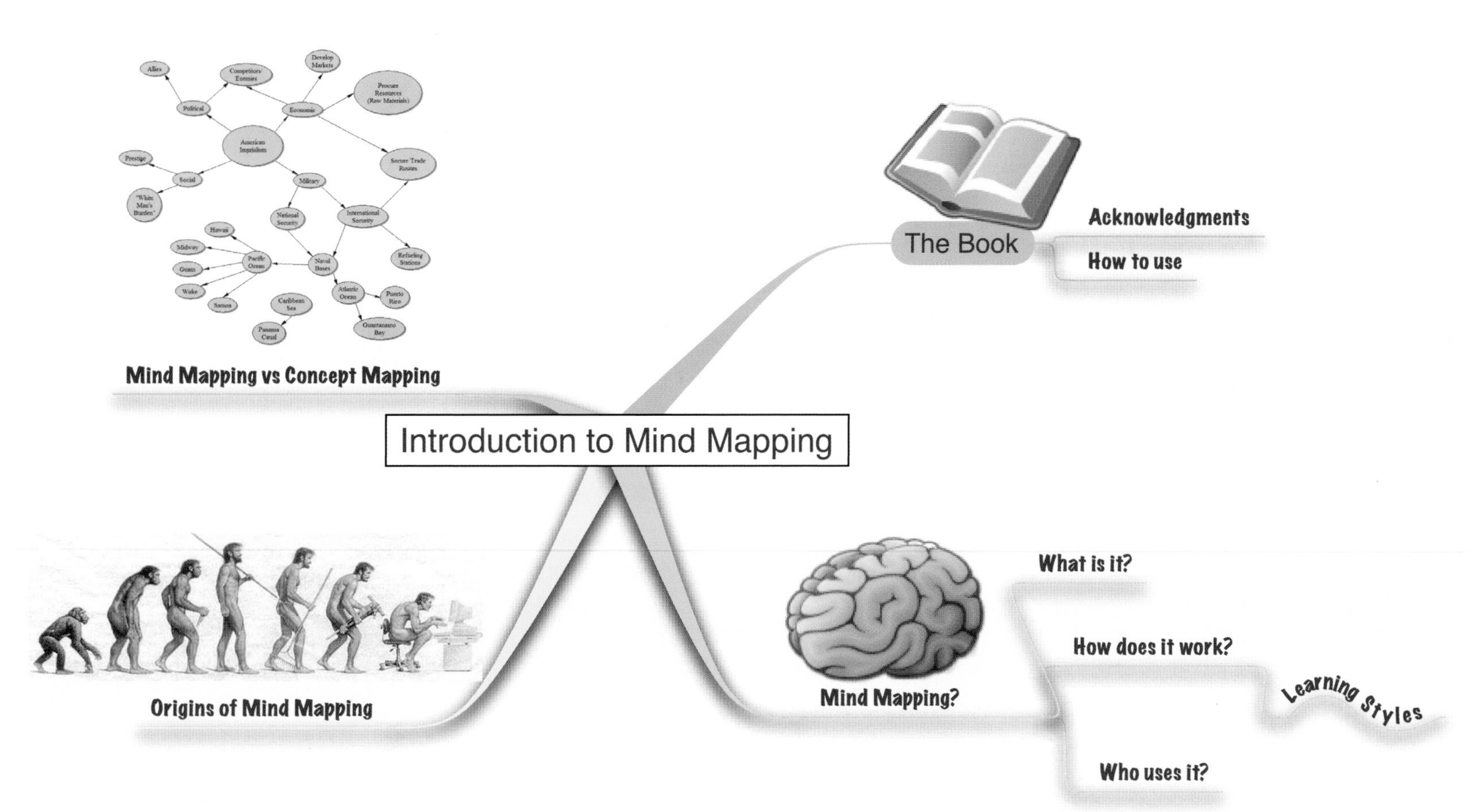

Acknowledgements

The author wishes to express gratitude to the following people for their invaluable assistance in compiling this book:

- The University of Minnesota, Digital Media Centre
- The Department of Education, Tasmania
- The Department of Education, Queensland
- The Australian Association for Teaching English
- Allan Luke and Peter Freebody
- Barbara Stauble
- Mark Gilchrist
- Hazel Wagner
- Craig Turner
- Margaret Rees
- Leela Cosgrove
- Dr. Marc Dussault

...and all the others who have helped with editing, reviewing, and providing moral support.

How To Use This Book

This book is split, roughly, into two parts.

The first four chapters concentrate mainly on theory – what Mind Mapping is, the studies that have been conducted that show why and how it is useful, the information on the benefits that Mind Mapping brings.

Chapters 5, 6 and 7 are more practical. They'll show you how to construct a Mind Map, how to choose the right software for your needs and will even give you some sample lesson plans that other teachers have used in their classrooms.

Chapter 8 contains a list of commonly used Mind Mapping and Personal Development terms along with information about the author, a range of online resources, and a list of Mind Mapping software applications that you can obtain for free if you want to 'try before you buy', so to speak. You will also find instructions there about how to be part of our exclusive book owners' forum on our web site, and gain access to electronic copies of Mind Maps used in this book, and a place to share ideas and lesson plans with other teachers.

As you work through each chapter, refer to the last page of the chapter where you'll find a template Mind Map. This template is for you to fill in with the ideas you have, distinctions you make and the information you pick up.

Yes, I want you to write in this book.

I know, for some of you, that's a scary proposition. But it will be OK. I promise.

Most importantly, these Mind Maps will give you a taste of what the process is all about. Personally, I think you'll be hooked! But if it's not for you, you should be able to tell fairly quickly from these simple exercises.

While I have attempted to define each of the terms associated with Mind Mapping within the text of this book, I have also included a 'Common Mind Mapping Terms' table at the beginning of Chapter 8 as a reference guide.

All of the Mind Maps in this book have been created using the Mind Mapping software, NovaMind.

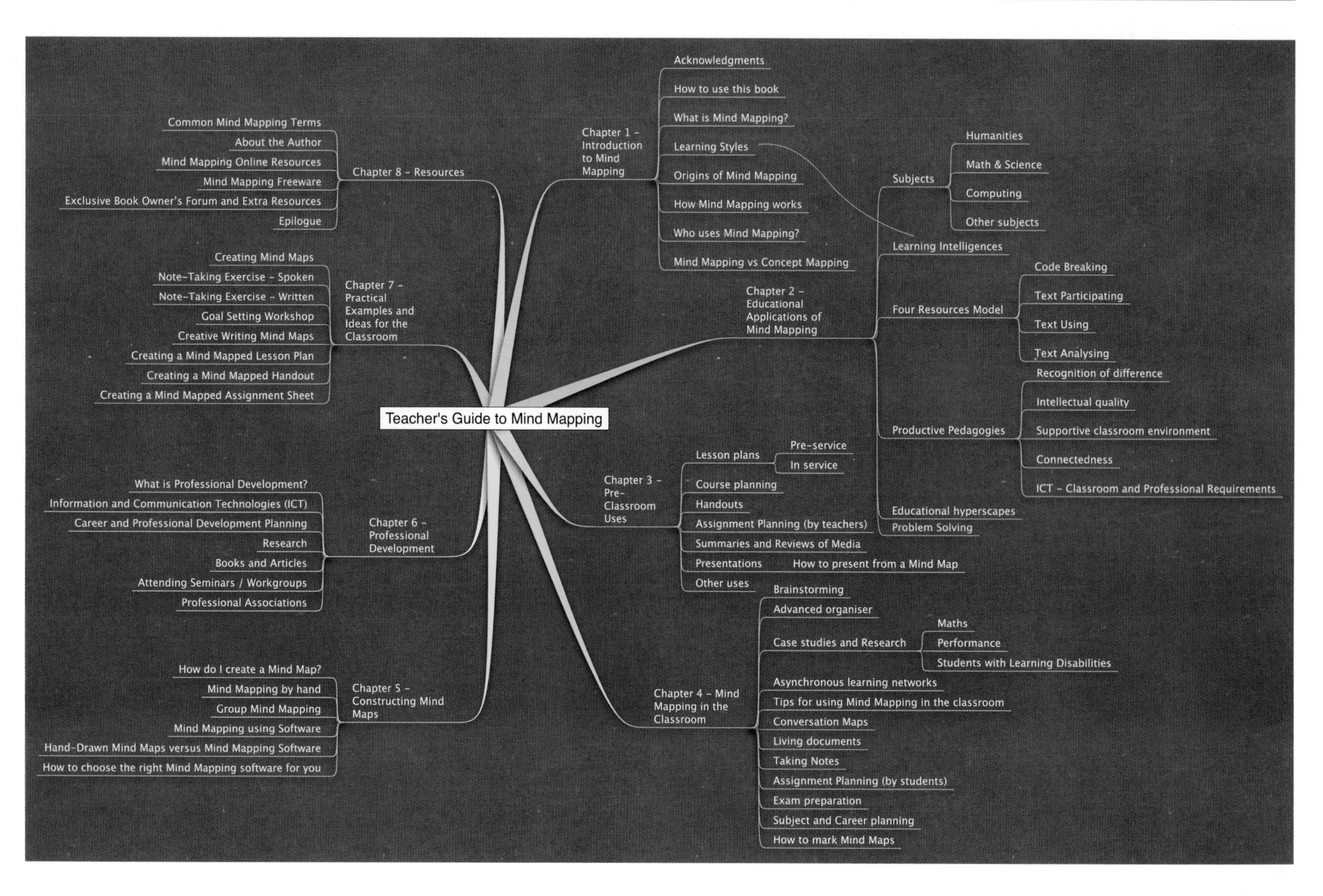
Teacher's Guide to Mind Mapping
Chapter 1 - Introduction to Mind Mapping
Acknowledgments
How to use this book
What is Mind Mapping?
Learning Styles
Origins of Mind Mapping
How Mind Mapping works
Who uses Mind Mapping?
Mind Mapping vs Concept Mapping
Chapter 2 - Educational Applications of Mind Mapping
Subjects
Humanities
Math & Science
Computing
Other subjects
Learning Intelligences
Four Resources Model
Code Breaking
Text Participating
Text Using
Text Analysing
Productive Pedagogies
Recognition of difference
Intellectual quality
Supportive classroom environment
Connectedness
ICT - Classroom and Professional Requirements
Educational hyperscapes
Problem Solving
Chapter 3 - Pre-Classroom Uses
Lesson plans
Pre-service
In service
Course planning
Handouts
Assignment Planning (by teachers)
Summaries and Reviews of Media
Presentations
How to present from a Mind Map
Other uses
Chapter 4 - Mind Mapping in the Classroom
Brainstorming
Advanced organiser
Case studies and Research
Maths
Performance
Students with Learning Disabilities
Asynchronous learning networks
Tips for using Mind Mapping in the classroom
Conversation Maps
Living documents
Taking Notes
Assignment Planning (by students)
Exam preparation
Subject and Career planning
How to mark Mind Maps
Chapter 5 - Constructing Mind Maps
How do I create a Mind Map?
Mind Mapping by hand
Group Mind Mapping
Mind Mapping using Software
Hand-Drawn Mind Maps versus Mind Mapping Software
How to choose the right Mind Mapping software for you
Chapter 6 - Professional Development
What is Professional Development?
Information and Communication Technologies (ICT)
Career and Professional Development Planning
Research
Books and Articles
Attending Seminars / Workgroups
Professional Associations
Chapter 7 - Practical Examples and Ideas for the Classroom
Creating Mind Maps
Note-Taking Exercise - Spoken
Note-Taking Exercise - Written
Goal Setting Workshop
Creative Writing Mind Maps
Creating a Mind Mapped Lesson Plan
Creating a Mind Mapped Handout
Creating a Mind Mapped Assignment Sheet
Chapter 8 - Resources
Common Mind Mapping Terms
About the Author
Mind Mapping Online Resources
Mind Mapping Freeware
Exclusive Book Owner's Forum and Extra Resources
Epilogue

What is Mind Mapping?

Mind Maps represent a task or idea in a pictorial form with a minimum of words. They rely on key pictures and words that act as 'triggers' to the person / people who have designed it and that will also resonate with people viewing it.

Simply put, a Mind Map is a visual representation of what's going on in your head. It lets you see, in one picture, the thoughts, tangents and ideas your brain connects to a particular concept.

As you can see from the diagram on the next page, the centre of the Mind Map is often a picture. This picture expresses the central concept of the Mind Map, whether it's a task that you need to perform, a presentation you are giving, a plan for a book you want to write or an outline of a book you've read, the Mind Map breaks down complex ideas into a series of logical and intuitive branches.

Each branch contains a major idea that supports the central concept and branches, further, to the minor ideas that support the major ones.

The use of colours helps you to visually associate ideas with colours - something our brains are very adept at doing, and this is further enhanced by the images. Where appropriate, including humour makes the Mind Map even more interesting so your brain really latches on to the concepts and remembers them.

By doing this, what may otherwise be a complex concept (such as explaining how Mind Maps work) can be broken down into a one-page outline that is easy to understand and digest.

In fact, it's taken me approximately 250 words (so far) to explain to you what the Mind Map conveys in seconds!

If you are not familiar with Mind Maps, the picture on the previous page may look a little strange. However, once you have grasped the basics of Mind Mapping you'll be producing much more involved Mind Maps of your own in next to no time!

In some circles, Mind Maps have gained a reputation as a 'new age' approach – with the accompanying insinuation that they are not altogether on the planet.

But really, Mind Maps are just about freedom.

They free you from rigid, structured, institutionalised thinking and allow you to approach issues with the freedom of creativity.

By Mind Mapping you move yourself – literally! – out of the box. You free yourself to think in pictures, in one word descriptions and relationships between ideas.

A Mind Map is like Willy Wonka's glass wonkavator – it can go up and down – but also sideways and slantways and longways and backways and frontways and squareways – any ways you like!

Mind Mapping won't necessarily be a concept that works for everyone. Debates rage as to whether it is a useful planning technique

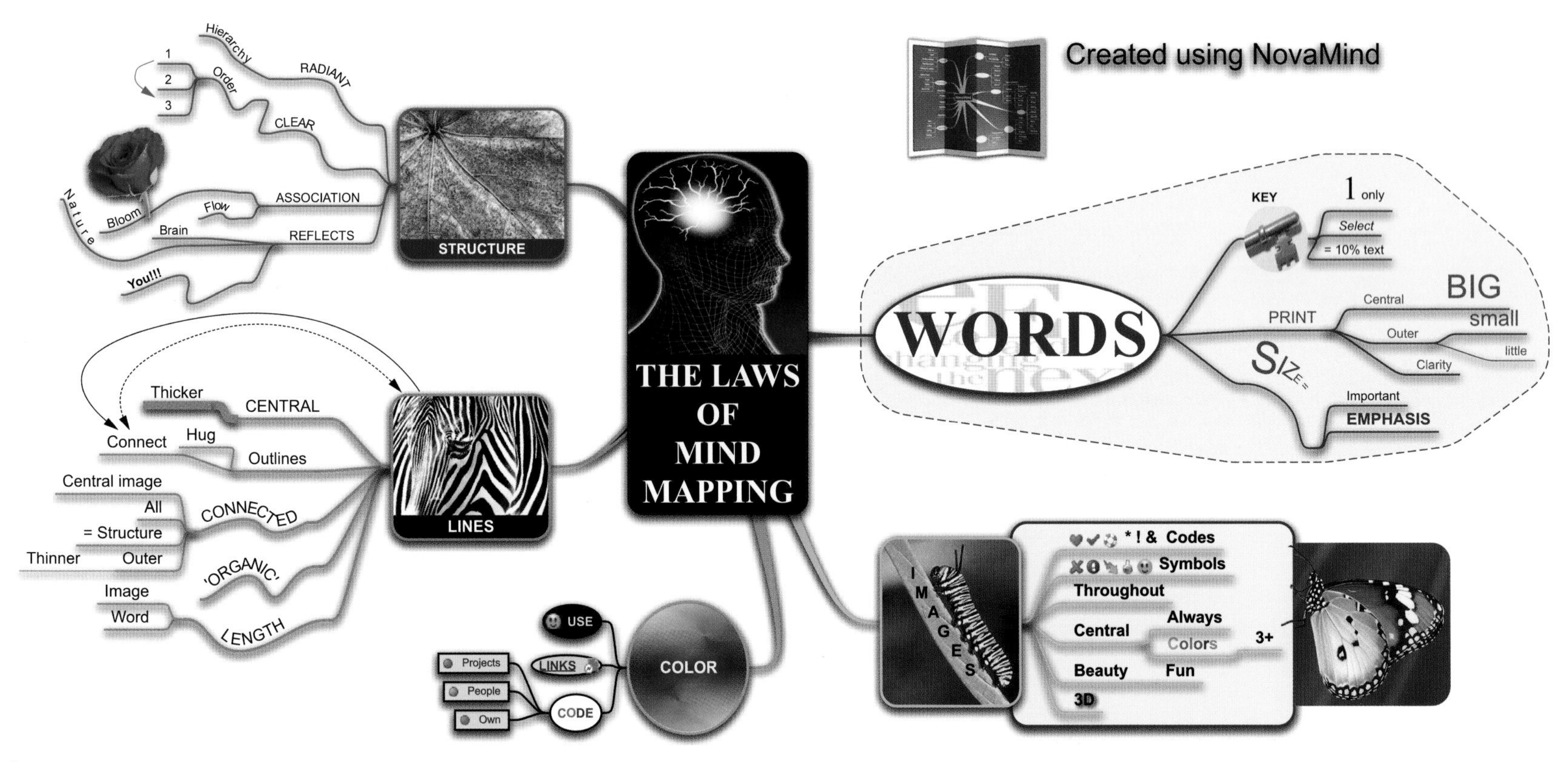

or a 'cobble of pop-psychology'. But the only person who can answer that question for you, is you. Many people swear by Mind Mapping as a tool they could never live without. They say it helps them to remember things and to organise their thoughts.

Having worked with Mind Maps for years, I've received hundreds of testimonials from people who are amazed by the difference Mind Maps have made in their lives. Personally – it has changed my life. It's helped me design the future that I want, plan it out and implement it, including helping me to create a highly successful Mind Mapping business.

But it's up to you to decide for yourself.

That's one of the main purposes of this book – to explain the concept of Mind Mapping, show its background, uses and what it can do and then to allow you to make your own choice as to whether this is a practice that you can fit into your life. I sincerely hope you will approach Mind Mapping with an open mind and that it will bring you the benefits and amazing insights that it has brought me!

The Different Learning Styles

Different people take in knowledge in different ways. The three major learning styles are classed as: Visual, Auditory and Kinesthetic.

- **Visual learners** – learn by seeing things. They prefer to have information described to them in diagram or pictorial form. They find it easier to interpret information from a teacher when they can see the teacher's facial expressions and body language.

- **Auditory learners** – learn by listening to things. They prefer to have information described to them by another person. They like to talk through problems to find a solution. They often have difficulty interpreting written information, preferring to read it out loud.

- **Kinesthetic learners** – learn by moving, doing and touching things. They prefer to have information described to them in a physical form. They learn best when they can 'get their hands dirty'. Kinesthetic learners often have trouble sitting still for extended periods of time.

Visual learners are particularly drawn to Mind Maps, however they have many benefits for auditory and kinesthetic learners as well. Auditory learners will

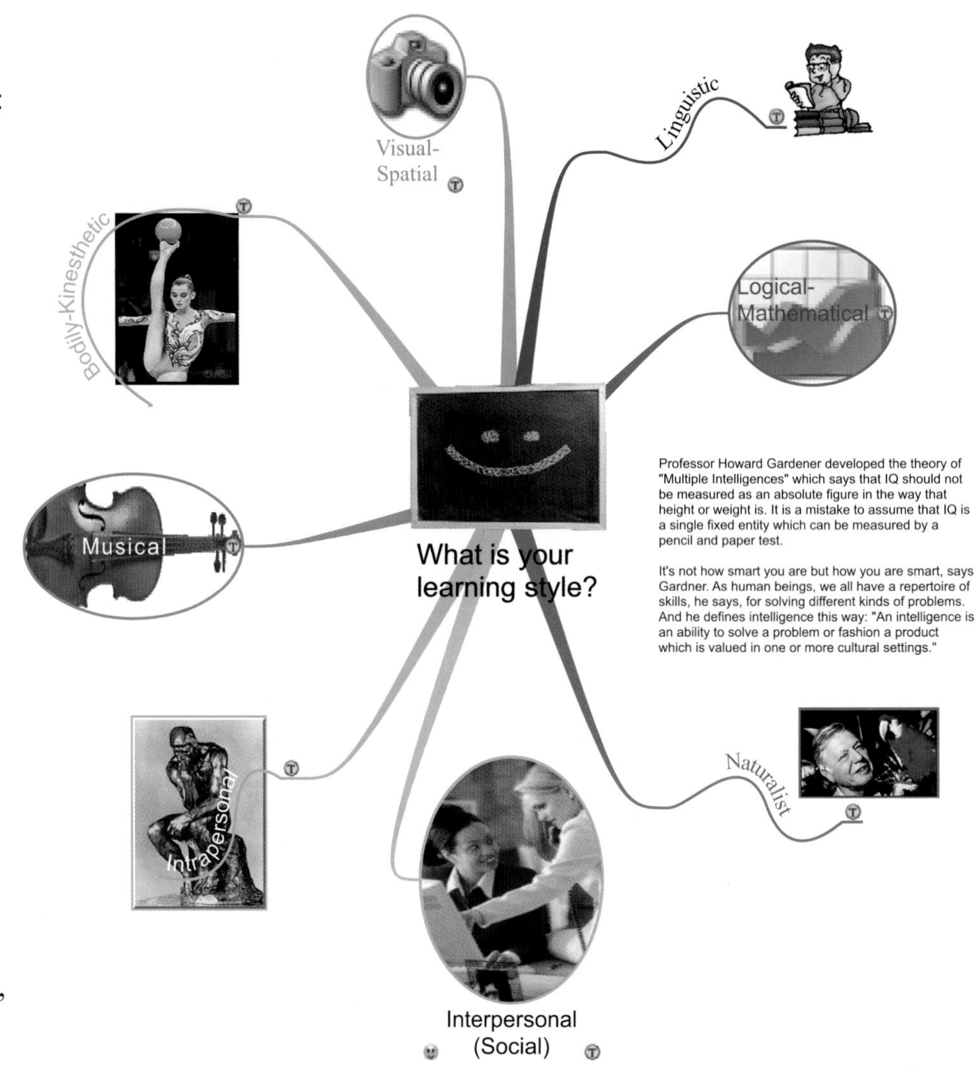

find that the simple layout of a Mind Map is far preferable to the jumble of words on a page. Kinesthetic learners will be impressed by a Mind Map's sense of movement and flow.

Basically, information is much more easily digestible for anyone when it is broken down in to small pieces. Mind Maps do just this, allowing all learning types not only to access information in a simplified form, but also making it easier for them to store and recall information.

Where does Mind Mapping come from?

The idea of Mind Mapping has been around, in one form or another, for thousands of years. It has been used in areas such as education, psychology and engineering.

It was formalised under the name 'Mind Mapping' by Tony Buzan, a University of British Colombia graduate with double Honours in Psychology, English, Mathematics and the General Sciences, who was inspired by Alfred Korzbyski's concept of General Semantics (technically defined as the "reaction of the whole human organism in its environment to some event — any event, not just perceiving a human-made symbol — in respect of that event's meaning"[1]).

Alfred Korzbyski's work also forms the foundations of some aspects of neuro-linguistics, and one thing that bridges the world of neuro-linguistics and Mind Mapping is his statement that "The map is not the territory", meaning that we all have internal representations of our version of reality that we work from, and in a Mind Mapping context, we are both representing this internal representation and challenging ourselves to extend and alter it to come up with better, more empowering solutions and more connections.

Since this incarnation of Mind Mapping was introduced by Tony, many excellent software products have become available that make Mind Mapping an even more simple and intuitive process.

1 *'General Semantics', Wikipedia, http://en.wikipedia.org/wiki/General_semantics*

How does it work?

A much more in-depth look at creating Mind Maps can be found in Chapter 5, but here is a brief overview of how to put a Mind Map together.

1. The first step is to distinguish your central concept. If you are using a Mind Map to take notes from a presentation, probably the title of the presentation is a good candidate for the title. Ditto if you are summarizing a book. If you are doing some research, you'll need to gather together your materials relating to this – research papers, text information, images that you may want to use, and decide on the best concept. Of course if you are using Mind Mapping software, you will be able to change it later if necessary.

2. Next, choose a word, phrase or (preferably) a picture to represent the central concept and place it at the centre of the page. Use dimension, expression and colours to attract attention and aid memory.

3. From here, you'll brainstorm your main, supporting ideas – or BOI's (Basic Ordering Ideas), these are the equivalent of categories or chapter headings and radiate out from the title. These are also often referred to as "top level branches".

4. Add supporting information in 'child' branches under the BOIs, with the most important closest to the centre.

5. Be sure to use images, branch shapes and graphic text wherever possible. Use your own coded colours to represent links and relationships between different ideas.

6. When in first draft, be sure to capture ideas as quickly as possible. Leave editing and reorganising, elaborating and clarifying for your second draft. If you are using a Mind Mapping application, the whole reorganization aspect becomes very easy.

Who uses Mind Mapping?

Mind Mapping has many applications – from note taking in a lecture to charting out your career path.

The following are some different ways in which different industries use Mind Mapping – there are many more than this, but this will give you an overall impression:

Education - Teachers

Improving Communication: As discussed earlier, different people have different methods of absorbing information and Mind Mapping can be an extremely useful tool for improving information retention in all different learning types and at different learning levels – from upper primary through to tertiary students.

You can print out the Mind Map and distribute it to students as a handout – whether the Mind Map is a summary of your lecture, of a book or research information, or succinctly makes your point in an easy to read and recall format.

Taking it a step further, when students are involved in the creation of a Mind Map during the presentation, this interactive method of teaching greatly improves the impact of the presentation, particularly on students for whom purely verbal lectures or paragraphs of written text are difficult to absorb.

The students hear the presentation for auditory learning, see the Mind Map, providing visual learning, and they gain kinesthetic learning through creation of the Mind Map. It also stimulates the "Auditory Digital" thinkers who have to mull things over and work out how things fit together to understand and memorize the information.

Lesson Planning: Many teachers use Mind Mapping as a tool to create lesson plans. This is particularly useful as the Mind Map allows you to see very quickly what you know about the subject and where there may be gaps in your understanding / knowledge.

Mind Maps are an excellent way to compile and sort your thoughts on a subject into a comprehensive plan that, on one page, you can easily use within the classroom environment.

For further details on how to use Mind Maps to plan lessons, see chapter 3.

Providing Students with Life Skills: In our modern society it is so easy for students (and teachers!) to be struck with a variety of 21st Century dilemmas, such as:

- *Information Overload*: the modern human accesses more information in one day than their ancestors did over the course of their life. It's easy to get lost in all of that information unless you have specific skills and tools for organising, visualising and prioritising it.

- *Fragmentation of Information*: with the information overload comes the fragmentation of information – a lack of understanding of how information relates to other information can be overcome through systems which integrate, connect and reflect.

- *Rapid Change*: the world is moving at a faster pace than ever before. To survive in this ever-changing landscape it is essential that all people know how to plan, control, and anticipate. Proactivity is vital to survival and success.

- *Complex Dilemmas*: be they moral, financial, theoretical, physical, mental or spiritual – we are all faced with increasingly complex dilemmas. In order to solve these problems we need to be able to organise our thoughts and the information that we already have, structure this so that we can understand it and critically analyse our position and our beliefs.

Mind Mapping is an effective tool to help people deal with all of these modern dilemmas.

Mind Mapping has been considered a type of advanced organiser. It can help you to get all of your thoughts out and on to paper, clearly outlining your prior knowledge and learning. From there these thoughts can be arranged and rearranged; stretched or shrunk, until you find the answer to your problem.

Delivery of your Presentation: The four-step method of presenting from a Mind Map:

1. Place the subject of your presentation at the centre of the Mind Map, using colours and graphics to make it stand out. This way, you are always focused on your central idea – even if you go off on a tangent whilst presenting, a glance at the page in front of you will refocus your thoughts;

2. As the introduction to your presentation, read the top level branches;

3. The body of your presentation consists of the detailed information from the sub-branches of your Mind Map;

4. As a summary, reinforce your message by re-reading the Mind Map's top level branches.

Students

Taking Notes: During the lecture, note the key points as they arise on the main branches of your Mind Map. When the teacher goes into more detail on a point, add sub-branches with appropriate keywords.

Where there are specific facts related to the branch, record them in the text attached to the branch. By the end of the lecture you will have a compact, yet complete, record of the entire lesson. This will enable you to easily recall the entire lecture at a glance.

Summarising Information: Mind Mapping also makes summarising research information easy.

Set up key headings about your subject and then add detail on the branches underneath as you extract the information you want from the text. By adding graphics and colours you'll make the information come alive on your Mind Map – making information retrieval easier down the track.

Mind Mapping Your Thesis: You can use Mind Mapping to brainstorm ideas for your thesis. Once you've decided on your topic, Mind Mapping simplifies the planning process by helping you to break down the concept into individual topics, sub-topics and possibilities of each. One of the best features of Mind Mapping is that it can easily be a 'living document', allowing updates that keep a track of where you are as well as research information and links.

Mind Mapping for Assignments, Exam Preparation & Memorisation:

Use a Mind Map to record the aims, requirements, research tools and ideas for an upcoming assignment. This helps you to break the project down into manageable chunks. Cross each accomplishment off your 'task list' as it is completed. This leaves less opportunity to overlook any key requirements.

Your Mind Maps become your study maps, summarising vast quantities of information. The use of interconnecting branches, colours, graphics and keywords promote retention of information. So, when you are sitting in an exam trying to remember a specific date or formula, the work you have done to link that date or formula to a picture or colour will prompt visualisation of your Map and the retrieval of the information.

Personal Effectiveness

Problem Solving: Mind Mapping can help you to plan and brainstorm in order to find solutions and alternatives to your problems.

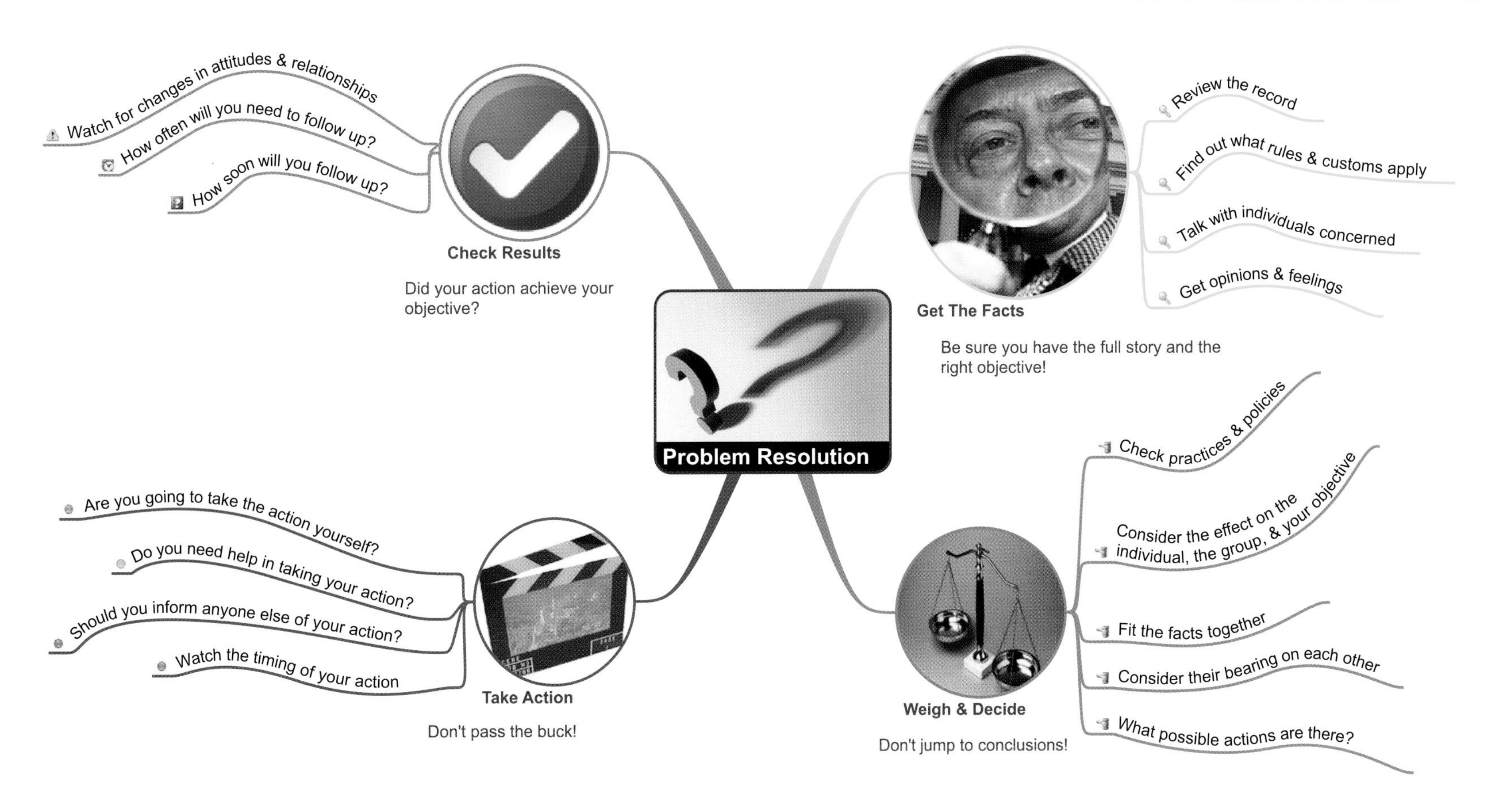

You can use a Mind Map like this as a stand-alone prompt mechanism so that you have a checklist to go through when you have a problem to solve. A more powerful use of this is to use it as a template, replacing the title with the challenge you are working on and altering the branches to suit your needs. Add extra branches and attach text to fill in the details of the problem and potential solutions. You can easily communicate your chosen resolution to other people using your Mind Map.

Once you tap into the flow of ideas you may find that they just keep coming!

Consider and compare the ideas you have documented and select the best options. Record further details under the preferred options, such as timeframes and the steps involved to achieve the desired outcome. Mind Mapping helps you tap into your ideas, identify solutions, stay focused and break problems down into manageable steps.

Plan Your Goals and Organise Priorities: Use key headings to represent short-term and long-term goals and priorities. Under each heading, list your strategies for success. You can also specify timeframes and defined milestones so you know when you have achieved your goal.

Including pictures of your goals in the Mind Map will help to keep you focused and motivated.

Career and Subject Planning: Whether you are employed, a University student or a high school student, Mind Mapping can help you plan out your future. By putting your ideal job / position in the centre and reverse engineering (see Chapter 4 for more information) your career, you can quickly and easily come up with a cohesive plan for your future.

Business

Brainstorming: Mind Mapping can be an excellent tool for use in brainstorming exercises. Whether you need ideas for marketing, KPI's, problem resolution or any of a host of business obstacles, using a Mind Map allows you, your partners and employees to free your thinking and come up with creative and innovative solutions.

Involving employees in these sessions is an excellent way to encourage them to 'own' the decision making process and their part in it. It also fosters creativity, initiative and improved relationships between management tiers within the organization.

Presentations: Mind Mapping is the perfect tool for planning and presenting. You can have a whole Mind Map on one page, detailing all the major points of your presentation and making it easy to follow – both for you and for the people you are presenting to – and ensuring discussions stay focused.

Mind Maps make excellent presentation handouts, improving the recall of information by the people you're presenting to – particularly if you use colours, graphics and links.

Many Mind Mapping programs will allow you to export directly to your presentation program, simplifying your presentation process even further!

Project Management: Project Management is a complex task that can require hours of meticulous planning and expensive software. Mind Mapping is used during the initial stages of the project to brainstorm the project goals and potential solutions. This provides a powerful way for the staff involved in planning the project to work together, building a definition of the problem that will be solved by the project. You use images, colour and shape to enhance the Mind Map, making it clear to everyone what ideas are related to each other, and the importance of the tasks.

From this you build a Mind Map with all the major tasks and their sub tasks identified on branches of the Mind Map, again using visual representations to identify task relationships and building clarity.

Everyone understands clearly the goals and tasks involved in the project because they can see how everything fits together visually. Further, some Mind Mapping programs are actually compatible with your project management software – allowing you to import from one to the other with relative ease.

Goal Planning: Defining, setting and working towards goals is as important for a company as an entity as it is for individuals.

People, be they employers or employees, feel most fulfilled in their work when they feel they are achieving something – using a Mind Map to plot and chart goals, for the company and for individuals within the company, increases staff satisfaction and gives them direction and inspiration. They can see why the goal is necessary, how all the tasks fit together and how they fit in and can contribute.

Mind Maps can even be used as an alternative to the traditional performance review documentation – allowing employees to chart their own career progress in a creative and dynamic format.

Selling your ideas: Whether you are an employee or employer, you would recognise that many businesses these days are risk-averse. It is increasingly difficult to 'sell' ideas – particularly if they are complex or require some level of explanation.

With a Mind Map you can break down complex ideas and make them simple – both for you to explain and for your client / boss / investors / employees to understand.

Whether you're developing a new product, trying to implement a new marketing idea or implementing changes to your company, Mind Maps will make your ideas more understandable and your objectives clearer to your audience.

By putting your key objective in the centre of your Mind Map and working the requirements for it out in logical branches, you can break down the most complex of ideas and overcome irrelevant objections.

Mind Mapping Vs Concept Mapping

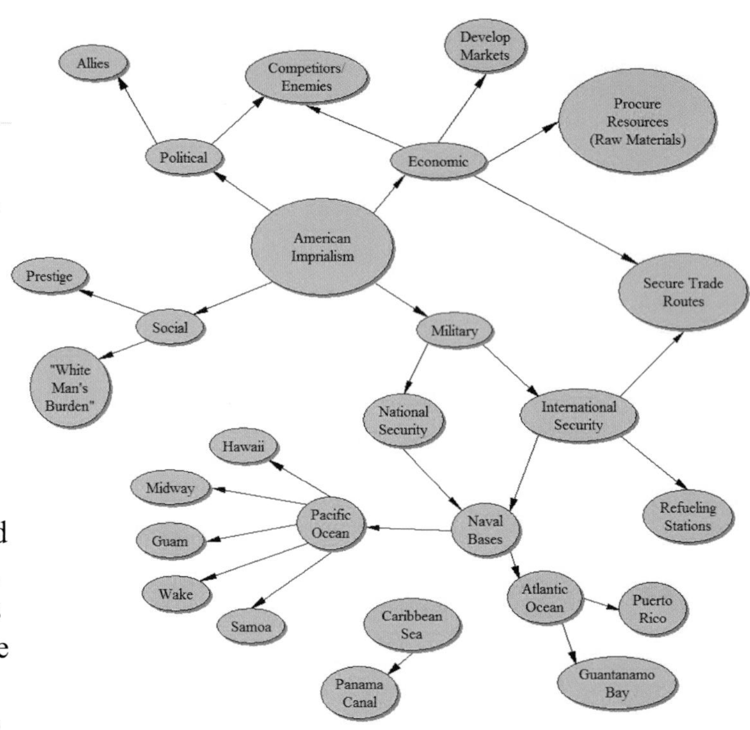

Confusion abounds in regards to the difference between Mind Mapping, Concept Mapping and other kinds of 'Mapping'. If you search for information on any of these terms, you'll find that one persons 'concept map' is another person's 'mind map'. To ensure that you won't be confused throughout the course of this book, I want to give you a short definition of Concept Mapping vs. Mind Mapping and why I feel that Mind Mapping is a vastly superior structure.

Simply put, a Concept Map differs from a Mind Map in that it has no central topic, does not use Radiant Thinking, has no single hierarchy and is therefore just a collection of graphical items with links between them. At the right is a Concept Map - actually quite a simple one, so it's not as difficult to understand as many Concept Maps are. You can see that there is no inherent hierarchy in the Concept Map. You could not definitively look at and know what it's all about - there is no 'title' - you just need to look at a number of the 'nodes' to try to work out what it is all about.

Similarly, you could not expect to be able to create an outline of the Concept Map - you would not know what order to put the topics in. This also prevents you from using it for project planning where there are tasks and sub-tasks.

A classic study done in 1969 demonstrated the importance of hierarchies as an aid to memory. Generating ideas with a Mind Map is much easier than making lists, because key words or "Basic Ordering Ideas" can be used as triggers for new ideas and associations.

In order for information to be recalled it must be "activated", and the level of activation depends upon the associative strength of the memory paths. The stronger the associative properties, the greater chance for the activation of the information being sought. The structures of Mind Maps are built upon this principle of creating strong connections between ideas.

The creation of a Mind Map reflects the logic of association of ideas in the same way that a neuron in your brain is a point from which associations go via the dendrites to other neurons, which in turn have many connections. Physically then, the brain is like the structure of a "concept map", where there are connections in all directions, but logically each particular topic is "radiant" in nature - that is, it has a central focus and radiating from that are the main ideas and radiating from them are the secondary ideas and so on.

Physically then, the brain is like the structure of a "concept map", where there are connections in all directions, but logically each particular topic is "radiant" in nature - that is, it has a central focus and radiating from that are the main ideas and radiating from them are the secondary ideas and so on.

Linear notes in the form of lists **directly oppose** the workings of the mind in that they generate an idea and then deliberately cut it off from those preceding and following it. This leads primarily to ideas being recorded in order of the time they were received rather than with what they logically relate to. Concept maps or cloud or cluster diagrams lose the structure and organization that maintains focus and ordering to the information.

By contrast, Mind Maps support memorisation, creativity and problem solving, as well as the logical layout of ideas and their relationships, through their radial connections and logic of association.

Mind Maps make information much more readily available for the mind to remember by highlighting it with colours, shapes and pictures, where Concept Maps are often dull and without adornment.

Mind Mapping is, in many ways, an evolved form of Concept Mapping – it takes the Concept Map to the next level. While some institutions still hold on to Concept Mapping, it is an outdated form of Mapping that has been usurped by Mind Mapping.

As this book goes on, you will note that some of the studies quoted refer to 'Concept Maps' instead of 'Mind Maps'. In some cases, this is due to the aforementioned confusion between the two. In other cases, this is simply a matter of the study having been conducted with a Concept Map.

Where the study has been conducted with a Concept Map, I would pose the question "If the study proves that Concept Mapping is a powerful and useful technique for teachers and students – how much *more* powerful would Mind Mapping be, since it adds **clarity**, **specificity** and **better defined structure** than Concept Mapping?".

This may be a question you wish to pose for yourself as you read on.

Mind Mapping is a skill that will serve you well regardless of where life takes you. It works as a road map, showing you the paths, permutations and progress of your journey to your goal.

Mind Mapping is not, as some may have you believe, a 'bunch of psycho-babble' or 'based on pseudo science'. In the next few chapters I have collected various studies by respected professionals from around the world that illustrate why Mind Mapping is useful and give examples of situations in which it has had excellent results for people in the educational field.

Of course, Mind Mapping is not the solution to all of the world's problems. It is not even the solution to all of your problems. Rather, it is a tool and a skill that, when properly applied and used in conjunction with other tools and skills, can help you to focus, think through and achieve your goals.

Mind Mapping may not be a tool that is suitable for everyone. However, studies show that it has at least some benefit for most people who use it, and many people find it immensely powerful and useful. Whether this benefit is ongoing or not, whether it is compelling enough for you or not, is for you to decide.

Now you can fill in the Mind Map on the next page with the information you learned.

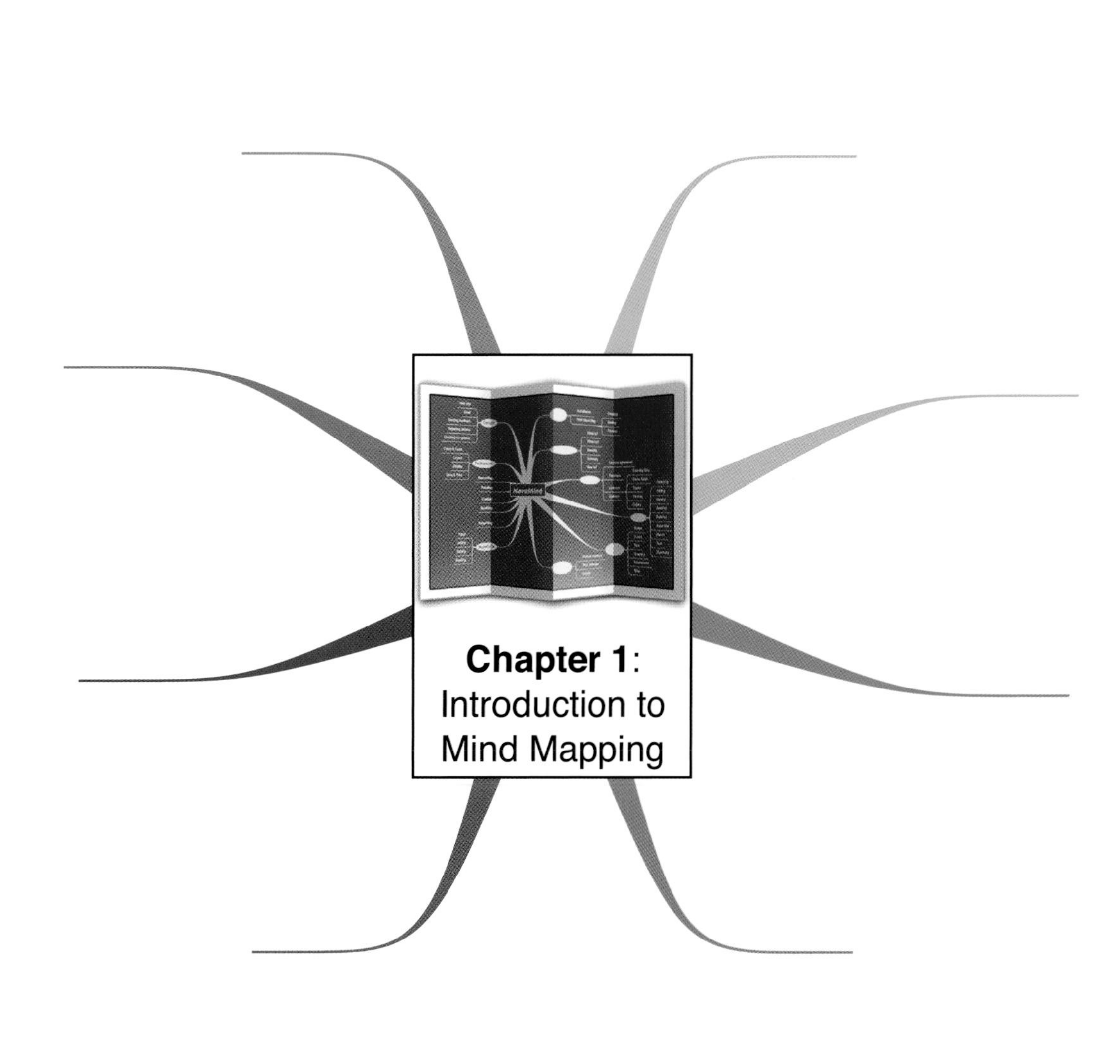

Chapter 1: Introduction to Mind Mapping

Chapter 2: Educational Applications of Mind Mapping

What use is a tool if you don't have any way to effectively put it into action? In this chapter, we will talk about some uses in specific subjects, and how Mind Maps hook in to the different learning intelligences and aspects of the "four resources model". We will examine "productive pedagogies" and see how Mind Maps provide support in this area too.

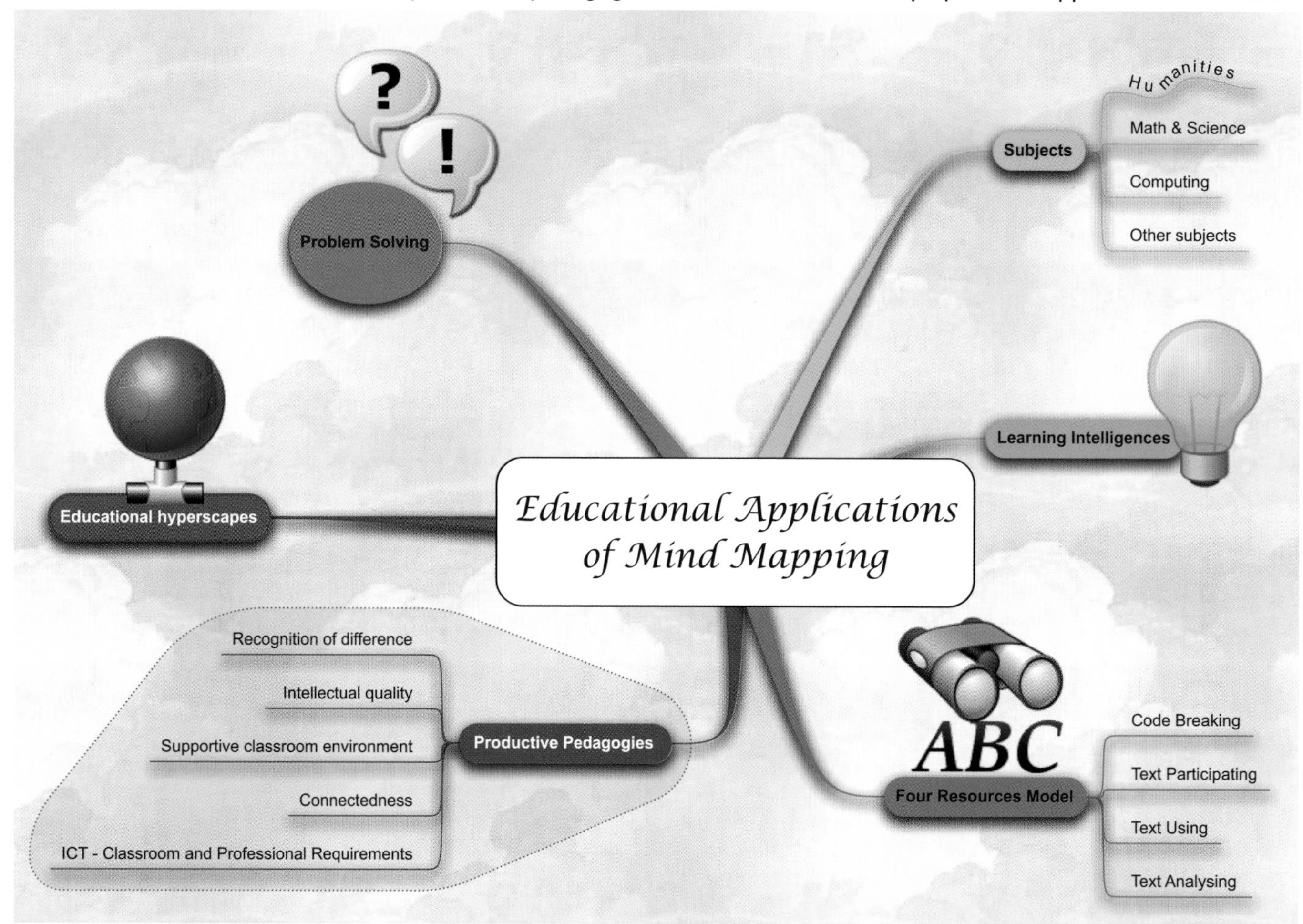

Educational Applications of Mind Mapping

Mind Mapping has many exciting possible applications for education. In no small part this is due to the ability of Mind Mapping to reach people at many different levels – regardless of learning style, educational level or subject being studied.

This chapter looks at some of the most important educational theories of the last few decades and discusses ways in which Mind Mapping simultaneously works with them all.

From different learning styles, to the Four Resources Model, to applications of Mind Mapping in different subjects, Mind Mapping's possible uses in relation to productive pedagogies and finally the new frontier of interactivity in online educational hyperscapes, this chapter will show that students, from primary to tertiary, can gain enormous benefits from learning the discipline of Mind Mapping.

Mind Mapping pushes the user to think about new and different ways of organising information. For too long students have been boxed into a stern ruling of 'how to' – write assignments, take notes – even creative activities are given a formula. We now know that this learning style works for only a small percentage of the population and may, in fact, be responsible for low marks, depression and, at its most extreme, school dropouts.

Mind Mapping requires logical and creative thinking – in fact, Mind Mapping teaches these at an incredibly high level because it forces students to discover these things for themselves. By drawing even a basic Mind Map a student is put in a position where they must think:

1. What is my central theme?
2. What main ideas support, challenge, or extend this?
3. How can the main ideas be broken down further or extended in new directions?

This chapter looks at some of the most important educational theories of the last few decades and discusses ways in which Mind Mapping simultaneously works with them all.

While, in some ways, this may seem no different to instructing students to write an introduction, body and conclusion plan, for many students the interactive and visual nature of a Mind Map will have far more beneficial results, allowing them to focus better, be more productive, come up with better solutions, and explore new concepts that they would not otherwise have thought of.

Applications for different subjects

Humanities:

The uses of a Mind Map as a planning technique for presentations and assignments is clear and is discussed in much greater detail in Chapter 4. However, Mind Mapping can be used for more than just planning assignments and presentations.

For example, a **History** teacher could create (or have students create) a Mind Map which represents all of the Chinese Dynasties on one page.

A **Geography** teacher could use a Mind Map as the basis for an assignment on the various effects of low levels of water fall over an extended period of time.

A **Theatre** teacher could have the students use a Mind Map to plan their major performance piece – helping them to sort out and organise all of the different facets of a performance that they need to take into account.

An **English** teacher could use Mind Maps to help students summarise the important themes from a novel that they have read.

Maths and Science:

Generally, the more complicated and in depth the information the more useful a Mind Map truly is. Maths and Science subjects can be incredibly involved. Students need to memorise a high volume of scientific data and formulae. They need to remember how things inter-relate. Such a vast amount of information can quickly get confusing.

However, using a simple Mind Map, complex ideas can be broken down into an easy to understand, one page document.

A study recently conducted in the Netherlands[1] found that students had a much easier time understanding Mathematics as a subject in context. That is, when students were taught the history of mathematics, they were better able to absorb the subject and were

1 *Netherlands Organisation for Scientific Research (2005), "Euclid returns to math lessons", December 15, 2005, http://agutie.homestead.com/FiLEs/mindmap/math_history_time_line.html*

much more interested and motivated than students without the background.

In fact, Van Gulik's research found that there were even correlations between the mistakes that students without this historical basis made and the mistakes made by the original developers of certain mathematical theories! By teaching students the background of a theory – giving them the 'why' and the 'how' rather than just a formula, they were able to more fully comprehend the way the formula works, and therefore better able to use it effectively and correctly. Representing the background and context on Mind Maps gives this strong context in which understanding is enhanced.

This is also a particularly useful theory for those students whose focus is more on the humanities – by incorporating history into the class they become more motivated and interested.

Computing:

Mind Mapping obviously works well for planning web pages – the layout is ideal for planning a dynamic and interactive hyperscape (see below for further information about hyperscapes).

However, Mind Mapping can also be useful in the development of computer programs and in explaining how computer systems and programs work. The inherent complexity of the topics can easily be broken down into a hierarchical format that is both easy to explain and easy to understand.

Other Subjects, Tertiary and other Education

There are many more uses for Mind Mapping throughout educational institutions – the applications are limited only by your own imagination. In my Mind Mapping software company (NovaMind) we get feedback telling us about university lecturers who use it for presenting their lectures, university students who Mind Map their lectures, assignments and theses, churches who use it for seminars, teaching and outreach programmes, and so on.

In fact, one of the difficult things with telling people about Mind Mapping is trying to explain what it is used for, because I keep hearing of more and more uses for it that I wouldn't have thought of before.

Learning Intelligences

The idea of 'different kinds of intelligence' is in no way new – it has been with us for many hundreds of years. However, when the idea of schooling as a necessity, rather than as a special privilege for the elite few, became prevalent, a very rigid structure was put into place to monitor the ways in which knowledge was imparted. While there have always been progressive schools and teachers who have embraced ideas that were considered to be 'outside of the box', it is only in the last twenty years or so that these ideas have really begun to find their way into the mainstream.

It is now widely accepted that a student who has problems with English isn't necessarily stupid, but rather may be less inclined to learning from a visual and auditory view point (the way in which English is traditionally taught). These students may therefore benefit from creating pictures or making models – some form of 'doing' exercise – rather than just reading a book or discussing it.

It is considered that there are, in fact, more than three learning styles. Others include: Musical Learners, Spatial Learners, Mathematical / Logical Learners, Interpersonal Learners and Intra personal Learners.

However, the three main learning styles, as detailed below, cover the majority of people.

Everyone uses a combination of learning styles, but normally students find that they predominantly engage in one of the following learning styles for maximum results:

Visual Learners: like to see what they are learning; find something to look at if they are bored; remember things by closing their eyes and visualising them; tend to be very neat; like to take a lot of very detailed notes; often choose to sit at the front of the class; enjoy written or spoken language that is very rich in detailed imagery; like handouts and presentations that use colour and pictures; enjoy learning environments that are isolated from distraction.

Auditory Learners: like to absorb knowledge by hearing it – whether from the teacher or reading out loud to themselves; remember things by repeatedly verbalising these things to themselves; like to talk to themselves; often choose to sit where they can hear best, regardless of where that is in a classroom.

Kinesthetic Learners: it is now coming to light that some students that have been diagnosed with learning disorders may actually be kinesthetic learners. Until recently, these kinds of students have had difficulty in many subjects, often excelling in less traditional subjects – such as wood work, graphics, home economics and catering. This is not due to an inability to comprehend more intellectually complex subjects such as maths, science and English but rather is due to the fact that kinesthetic learners are uncomfortable with traditional classroom structures, preferring situations where they can manipulate materials and move around. Kinesthetic students often have trouble sitting still for an extended period of time. They like to express themselves physically and enjoy subjects such as art and physical education.

The Four Resources Model

On its web page, discussing literacy, the Department of Education Tasmania[2] says:

> *"Literacy is no longer viewed as a single, finite 'thing', but rather as a flexible repertoire of skills, strategies and practices that are closely linked to context and purpose. Contemporary views of what it means to be literate have moved beyond print literacy to encompass notions of active citizenship, new communication practices and information technologies, critical thinking and linguistic and cultural diversity. The multiplicity of literacy practices has led educators to use the term multiliteracies to emphasise the diverse ways that we use the communication practices of the world in which we live.*
>
> *Literate students access the resources involved in being a competent communicator and use these resources in interconnected ways with the focus always on making meaning and communicating. These resources include working with the codes in which texts are constructed, participating in making meaning of texts, using texts for different purposes, audiences and contexts and critically analysing and transforming texts."*

This quote is an excellent summation of the concept behind the Four Resources Model, where literacy is broken down into four essential parts for analysis, comprehension, involvement, and usage of language. The breaking down of the teaching of literacy into these parts has the potential to pinpoint areas where a student may be having difficulty, and in the old schooling system have missed

2 *Department of Education Tasmania Website, (2006), Specific Focus, Principles and Practice, http://www.ltag.education.tas.gov.au/focus/beingliterate/princprac.htm*

out in one aspect of their learning, meaning that the other parts which they did understand would not be utilized and they would fall behind in their education. This often leads to a wider impact on their overall understanding across the curriculum, which could also lead to loss of interest in education, and therefore increased behavioural problems and other flow on effects.

In an update to their original discourse on the Model, Allan Luke and Peter Freebody[3] say:

> *"...we do not view how to teach literacy as a "scientific" decision, but rather as a moral, political and cultural decision about the kind of literate practices that are needed to enhance peoples' agency over their life trajectories and to enhance communities' intellectual, cultural and semiotic resources in print/multi-mediated economies. Literacy education is ultimately about the kind of society and the kinds of citizen/subjects that could and should be constructed. Teaching and learning just isn't a matter of skill acquisition or knowledge transmission or natural growth. It's about building identities and cultures, communities and institutions. And 'failure' at literacy isn't about individual skill deficits - it's about access and apprenticeship into institutions and resources, discourses and texts."*

The Four Resources model discusses four resources that students require in order to be literate and be able to effectively use the literature that is available and create their own literature which is able to effectively communicate with others. This capability of effective communication flows from the text level through to the wide range of multimedia commutation means that are employed in education and society.

These Four Resources are defined as Code Breaking, Text Participating, Text Using and Text Analysing.

Code Breaking: is 'cracking the code' of communication. It takes into account the way print looks on a page, pictures, correct spelling, recognition of letter-sound relationships and even the codes of multimedia, such as camera angles and moving images. Every form of communication has its own context, vocabulary, and embodiment of the communication styles and emotional state of the author or presenter at the time. Breaking this code is essential to effective receipt of the communication.

Text Participating: is about the students personal responses to text – both through comprehension of existing texts and composition of their own, new texts. It asks students to compare their own life experience to what the author is conveying and to draw

3 *Luke, A and Freebody, P, (1999), "A Map of Possible Practices: Further notes on the four resources model", Practically Primary, Volume 4, Number 2, June 1999*

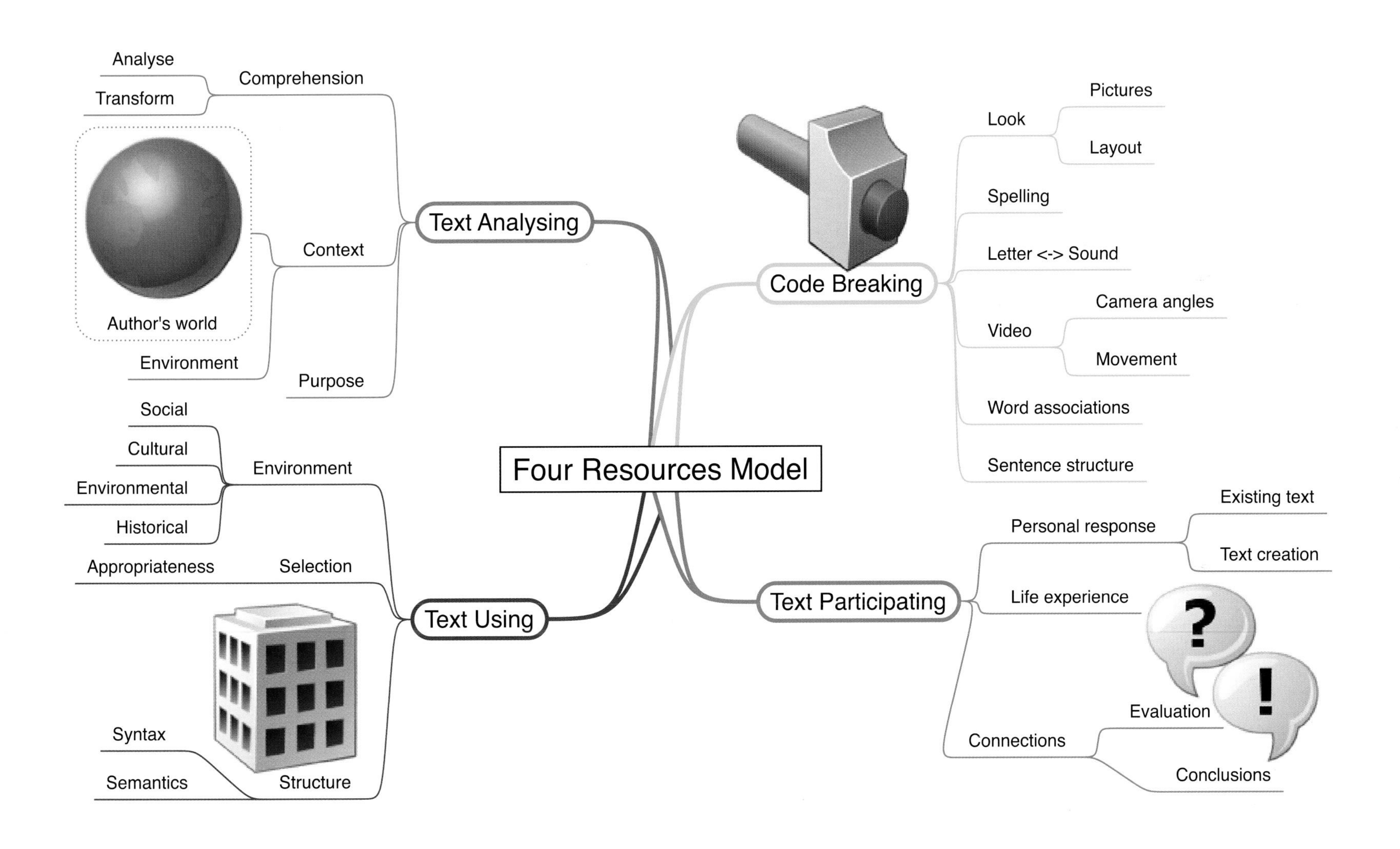
Four Resources Model
Text Analysing
Comprehension
Analyse
Transform
Context
Author's world
Environment
Purpose
Code Breaking
Look
Pictures
Layout
Spelling
Letter <-> Sound
Video
Camera angles
Movement
Word associations
Sentence structure
Text Using
Environment
Social
Cultural
Environmental
Historical
Selection
Appropriateness
Structure
Syntax
Semantics
Text Participating
Personal response
Existing text
Text creation
Life experience
Connections
Evaluation
Conclusions
?
!

conclusions on that, based on their own knowledge. It teaches students to make connections when comparing texts and to predict and evaluate the information they gather.

Text Using: deals with how students use the text they have comprehended / composed. This requires them to first understand the text – it's social, cultural, economic and historical relevance. It asks students to distinguish different kinds of language appropriateness for different situations and then applying that appropriateness to their own work.

Text Analysing: is about comprehension. It is the ability to critically analyse and transform texts. It requires the student to take into account that a writer is not neutral but rather colours their work, either directly or indirectly, with their own beliefs and opinions. This resource is about teaching students 'Don't believe everything that you read'.

What is the relevance of Mind Mapping to the Four Resources Model?

Mind Mapping can be a useful resource at each point of the Four Resources Model.

Code Breaking: A Mind Map is a powerful tool for breaking the code of communication. It allows the student to break down the text into its component parts and examine the structures inherent in it, mapping the text conventions and construction to understand the semantics of the intended communication.

Not only can a Mind Map be used as a tool for breaking other codes but it is, in and of itself, a kind of code. In fact, due to the high level of subjectiveness in its physical construct (regardless of an authors opinions, a book is always a book; a newspaper or magazine column is always set out the same) as well as its make up, it actually takes the idea of code breaking to a new level.

To decipher a Mind Map, the code breaker must take into account the central theme and then look at the main supporting ideas. Are these ideas correct? Are they really the Main Ideas, or should they have been demoted? What is the inherent logic the person who has compiled the Mind Map used? And what does it say about them and their background, knowledge of the subject, and ways of codifying the information for consumption by others (which also gets into the territory of Text Analysing too)?

Text Participating: Mind Mapping is an intensely personal exercise (personal to the individual or the group creating it) and encourages active participation in its creation. It is ideal for comparing texts – either through separate Mind Maps of each text or on one integrated comparative Mind Map. Further, some Mind Mapping software programs provide an option that, when activated, will provide word definitions and suggest alternate words that may also be useful. This allows the student to really take ownership of the material once they have broken the code as above.

When using Mind Maps to work with existing texts, the personal nature of the Mind Mapping process allows for the fitting of the new material being studied in to the student's world view and life experience, allowing them to see existing connections and find new connections which would not be apparent with any other form of analysing the material. They break down text information into single words and phrases, and then represent both the information and associations in a way that fits with their world and reflects their emotional and intellectual response to the material.

Text Using: Mind Mapping gives a much stronger meaning than prose, as it focuses on the keywords and semantic associations rather than the syntax, giving a rich meaning and focus on the best ways of representing the concepts for both personal consumption and sharing. This makes effective communication easier, either through the use of Mind Maps directly or by using Mind Maps to map out the structure and intent of the communication, and then taking that as a framework on which to hang the detail of the material being communicated.

Most Mind Mapping software assists with this by letting the student attach as much text to the branches of the Mind Map as they like so that they can have a uncluttered structure as well as the detailed content to work with, and they can reorganize the text just by reordering the branches. Also most Mind Mapping software allows for the student to create hyperlinks on the branches to resources like other local files or web pages. Some Mind Mapping software even goes further in the suggestion of possible words and associations that the student may not have thought of, often extending their vocabulary and the richness of their communication.

Text Analysing: Mind Mapping also helps students analyse the text in its entirety. By summarising the main themes of the text around its central concept students can begin to look at what those themes are, how the author has communicated them and whether they have achieved their intended goal. There are often many ways that authors colour their presentation of the material (either consciously or unconsciously), and using Mind Maps allows the students to understand more of the author's world, background, and emotional state at the time of writing, and build their own persuasive skills to present the information in the way that best represents their purpose at the time.

Productive Pedagogies and Mind Mapping

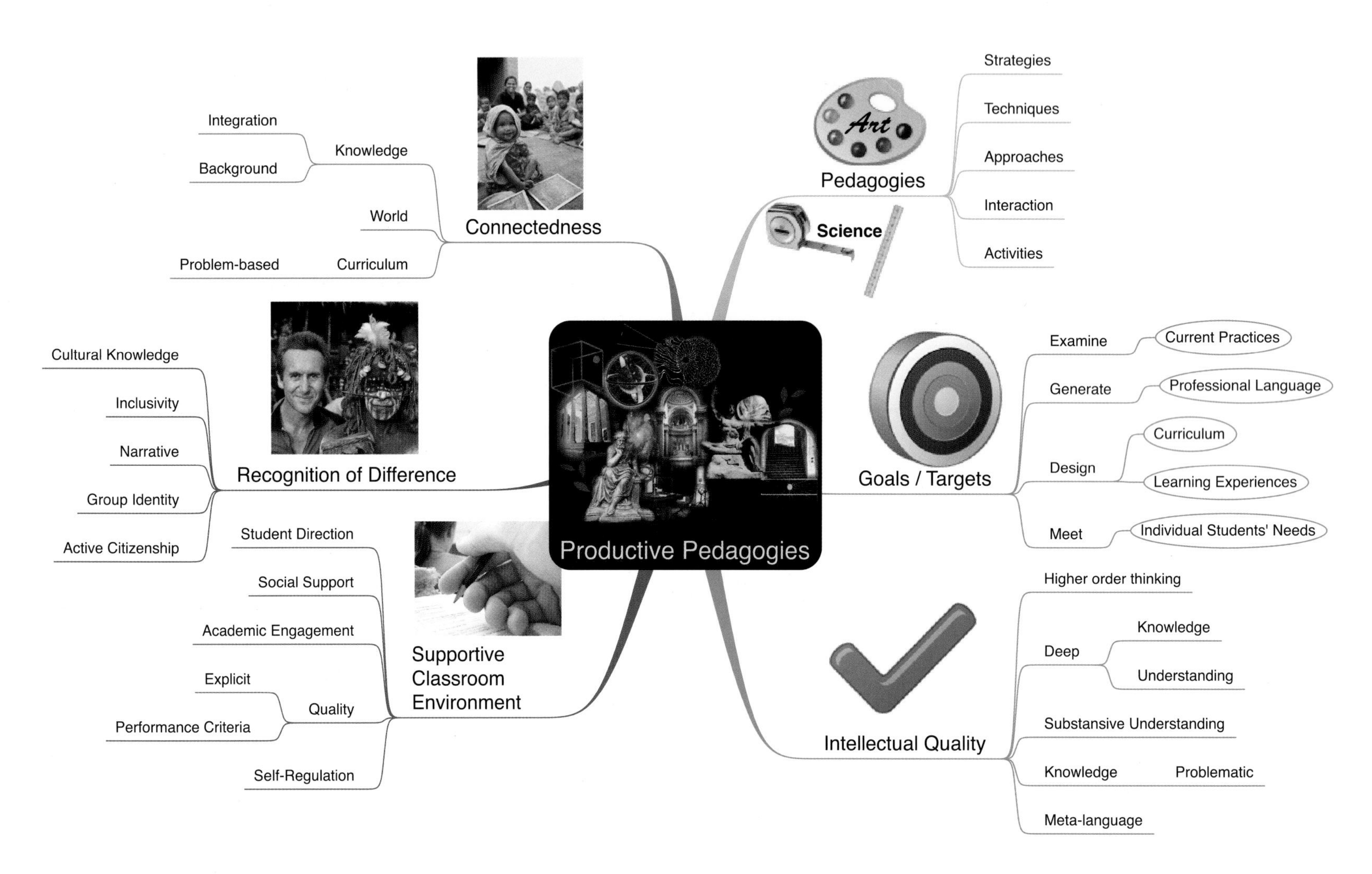

'Productive Pedagogies' is a balanced theoretical framework enabling teachers to reflect critically on their work. The Introduction to Education Queensland's *"A guide to ... Productive Pedagogies: Classroom reflection manual"*[4] says:

> *"Teachers should use the Productive Pedagogies framework to consider:*
>
> - *Are all the students I teach, regardless of background, engaged in intellectually challenging and relevant curriculum in a supportive environment?*
> - *How do my teaching and assessment practices support or hinder this?*
> - *What opportunities do I have to critically reflect upon my work with colleagues?"*

Recognition of Difference: Mind Mapping is inherently cross-cultural due to the limited nature of text required. Even where words are used, pictures can supplement them, making the Mind Map understandable regardless of potential cultural barriers. Culturally significant colours bring extra meaning and impact to the Mind Maps.

Mind Mapping is narrative based. However it is a non-linear, self-logical narrative, as opposed to traditional narrative structures. This gives students freedom to explore and play with the structures, bringing to it their own cultural narrative style and their own personal narrative style.

Inclusivity and group identity are encouraged by the use of Mind Maps as a group activity.

Intellectual Quality: Both deep understanding and deep thinking require students to not only be able to regurgitate the information they have learned, but to be able to take that knowledge and apply it in context. Mind Mapping assists with this by requiring students to re-group information in a different way to that in which it was learned, and to fit it with their existing knowledge base. This is particularly useful if the students are required to self-group the information rather than using groups predetermined by their teacher – something that comes naturally with computer based Mind Mapping.

Mind Mapping can be a useful tool for substantive conversation, helping the teacher to allow a free-flowing discourse that doesn't stray too far from its intended topic. The Mind Map can be used as a Conversation Map, keeping the discussions focused and on

4 *The State of Queensland Department of Education (2002), "A guide to ... Productive Pedagogies: Classroom reflection manual", http://education.qld.gov.au/public_media/reports/curriculum-framework/productive-pedagogies/*

course. Further, if the Conversation Map is able to be added to (as is the case using Mind Mapping software), it can grow to become a record of the conversation for later reference. This supports the effective communication of intellectual substance, the sharing of ideas in a free-flowing way, logical extension and synthesis of existing understanding, and sustained exchanges that go beyond the IRE (initiate / response / evaluate) pattern into more involved and substantive conversations with all parties evolving the structure and content of the discussion within the framework of the topic under consideration.

Supportive Classroom Environment: Mind Maps can be used to encourage student direction and academic engagement as a tool in which students are asked to have a level of input into their own learning. The level of engagement with the students is raised by the use of Mind Mapping in this way, while increasing the quality of the information exchange and level of understanding and retention by the students.

This can even be taken a step further and Mind Maps could be used as a tool for students to brainstorm and record their own subjects, goals and career paths (more on this in Chapter 4).

Connectedness: Connectedness is the central concept behind a Mind Map. Each has a central concept from which all other ideas radiate outwards – each idea is connected to the central concept and many of the ideas are independently connected to one another. In addition to connection from a knowledge perspective, the use of Mind Maps builds a stronger connection between the teacher and students, and encourages stronger bonds between the students as they see the Mind Maps that their peers have made and collaborate on Mind Maps together.

One of the concepts of productive pedagogies is a problem based curriculum. This is an ideal space in which to use Mind Maps. For thousands of years, Mind Maps have been used as a problem solving tool. While, as evidenced, they are useful in a broad range of applications, Mind Maps excel in the areas of brainstorming and problem solving.

ICT – classroom and professional requirements

An ICT framework is considered incredibly important in the modern classroom – both at a teaching and at a professional level. Teachers are expected to be life-long learners who keep themselves abreast of the latest technologies in order not only to utilise them but also to ensure that they are able to pass on technology information to their students in a confident and self-assured manner.

In fact, Education Queensland's "Smart Classrooms Professional Development Framework"[5] requirements for the "ICT Pedagogical Licence Advanced" include comments such as:

> *"I experiment and innovate with new ICT and teaching and learning methodologies to meet individual learning needs and to develop students' higher order skills and creativity;*
>
> *I create challenging tasks that integrate learning areas and involve student ICT use throughout all stages of the learning process and for a range of purposes;*
>
> *I set my own short and long term ICT learning goals based on regular reflection of my own professional practice and determined needs. I devise a plan and timeline to achieve these; and*
>
> *I am a lifelong learner who continually develops and expands my operational skills, conceptual knowledge and appropriate attitudes and behaviour towards the uses of ICT in educational settings"*

Mind Mapping can easily be applied to all of these areas. It excels as a professional development tool – from planning and time-lining your personal, professional goals through to the actual use of Mind Mapping software as an ICT tool for both you and your students. The applications clearly extend from the use of Mind Maps as a basic planning tool to the creation of "challenging tasks that integrate learning areas and involve student ICT use throughout all stages of the learning process and for a range of purposes". Using Mind Maps as an ICT exercise will develop and expand your operational skills, conceptual knowledge and appropriate attitudes and behaviour.

Teaching online, interactivity and hyperscapes

In their October 2000 paper "Handling hypermedia complexity: Fractal hyperscapes and mind mapping"[6], Bidarra, J., Guimarães,

5 *Education Queensland, Smart Classrooms, "Professional Development Framework, ICT", http://education.qld.gov.au/smartclassrooms/pdf/pd-framework.pdf*

6 *Bidarra, J., Guimarães, N., & Kommers, P.A.M. (2000). "Handling hypermedia complexity: Fractal hyperscapes and mind mapping", paper presented at the eighth ACM Multimedia Conference, Los Angeles, http://www1.acm.org/sigs/sigmm/MM2000/*

N., & Kommers, P.A.M. argue that the benefits of hypermedia are not yet being fully recognised and while this may have improved over the past six years the kind of full interactivity they discuss is still far from common place.

The authors say:

> *"...we concentrate on producing a lecture on video and put it on the Web so everybody can watch the presentation; we tend to forget that the Web is not a classroom and that the communication effects are very different – the Web is essentially an interactive medium not a TV channel..."*

Many learning institutions have still not grasped the full possibilities of the web. Some universities hold online tutorials – but these tend to consist of simple posting boards which may alienate students due to the vast amount of information that can be placed on them and, more importantly, the unorganised format of this information. Trying to find the information you are looking for or a conversation you've been having can be like looking for a needle in a haystack.

The ideal online learning environment is wholly interactive. It consists of web-based learning tools, response tools etc.

Online learning environments could learn much from social networking sites such as myspace and youtube. These sites are very user friendly, are easy to navigate and allow the user a great deal of control over their virtual environment. Users can customise the way they see and record information.

So, how does all of this fit in with Mind Mapping? Mind Mapping is an excellent collaborative tool that could easily flourish in an online learning environment.

For instance, for a small online class, a Mind Map could be set up by an online lecturer and students could add their own thoughts, insights and distinctions to it as the lecture progressed. This would not only benefit students from a collaborative and learning retention point of view, but would also allow lecturers to see, in real time, whether the information they are attempting to impart is being correctly interpreted.

Mind Maps would also make an excellent online tutorial tool. They could be used firstly as a plan of the tutorial and then as a note taking device for students and lastly an overall Mind Map could be drawn up by the tutor to record, with everyone's input, the discussions and outcomes of each tutorial.

One of the most fascinating concepts of online tutorials is the freedom that they provide. Students are not hampered by social restrictions – by fears of being judged or of the right or wrong answer. They are free to truly explore a subject in a fairly anonymous manner. Using Mind Mapping to record this journey serves to cement the amazing insights that they will gain for future reference.

Mind Mapping works with the idea that knowledge is not something that passively 'happens' to a person, but is rather the meeting of many ideas that a person actively chooses to take upon themselves. Mind Mapping illustrates that no matter how much information you put to how many students, each will have their own interpretation. Their interpretation will be based on many things – life experience, learned responses, mental issues – positive or negative. Information is not learned in the way a teacher intends but is absorbed in the way a student experiences it. In this way, information is a living creature – it evolves, twists, changes and transforms as it moves from person to person. All the rules and formulas in the world cannot change this. A human being is not a computer.

For a long time this had been seen as a theory that mainly applied to tertiary (and, to a lesser extent, upper secondary) students, as they necessarily have more control over their learning inputs and outcomes.

However, this theory is now extending to primary and secondary students. By involving students in the learning process in an active way, rather than heaping passive information on them and expecting them to learn by rote, we are entering an exciting new era in education. An era in which students of all ages become responsible for their own educational journey from a young age. An era in which students are taught that they are privileged to have access to vast amounts of knowledge and given the tools to utilize the information effectively.

Problem Solving

In our modern world it can sometimes feel like we do nothing but solve problems. We are faced with complex decisions on a daily basis. Without the systems, skills and tools to solve problems we would be adrift in a world that requires proactive and quick decisions in order to capitalise on opportunities and overcome hurdles.

While applicable to many different situations, Mind Mapping truly comes into its own when it is applied to problem solving as it is useful through the whole range of steps in the problem solving process.

Problem solving *is* a process. Mind Mapping is a tool to assist in that process. In Chapter 1, we saw the four step method of solving problems:

- Get the facts
- Weigh and decide
- Take action
- Check results

Putting this into practice in practical problem resolution makes for an effective framework to achieve successful results. Using Mind Maps for this also often opens up possible solutions or uncovers hidden causes that may have otherwise gone undiscovered. The first step in the process is to collect and organise the thoughts and the information that we already have. Using a Mind Map, we may look at factors such as:

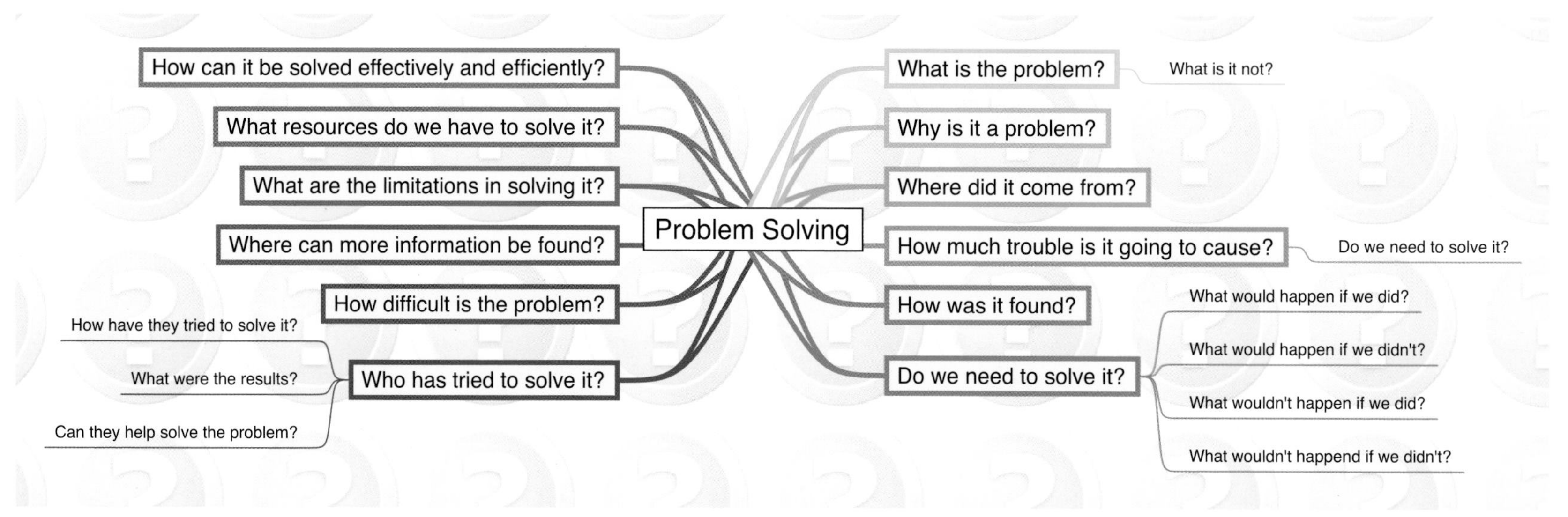

Next, you will need to structure these thoughts and references. How much of this information is important? How much of it irrelevant? How much of it is fact, as opposed to opinion or fear? You can colour code your Mind Map to indicate the relative importance of different factors, or use different adornments on the branches to show priorities or other attributes that are common across multiple branches.

The Map could then be shared with students, colleagues, peers, family and / or friends to help with feedback, before arriving at a conclusion.

In planning and taking action, and following up with checking the results, you can reuse the relevant portions of the Mind Map created when gathering the information and analysing it at the start of the process.

Mind Mapping is a useful tool at each step of the process of problem resolution. It can help you to clearly define your problem, where it came from, the issues it will cause, who can help you solve the problem and what resources are available.

Further, if you are using a software program, the Map can then become a reference tool – by hyper-linking branches to the resources they belong to (be they web sites or files in your hard drive) you begin to create a 'problem solving database'. The next time the same, or a similar problem occurs, you have a fully referenced answer that is only a click away.

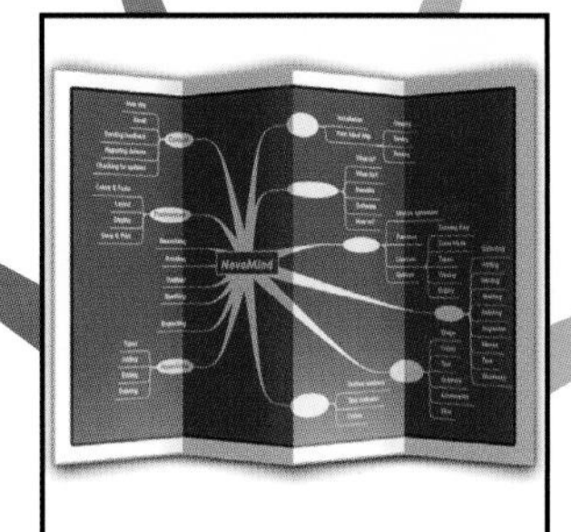

Chapter 2: Educational Applications of Mind Mapping

Chapter 3: Pre-Classroom Uses

In this chapter we will look at some of the ways you, as a teacher, can use Mind Mapping outside the classroom to research and prepare for your lessons quickly and effectively, and be able to present the information to your students in a way that is easy for you and captivating for them.

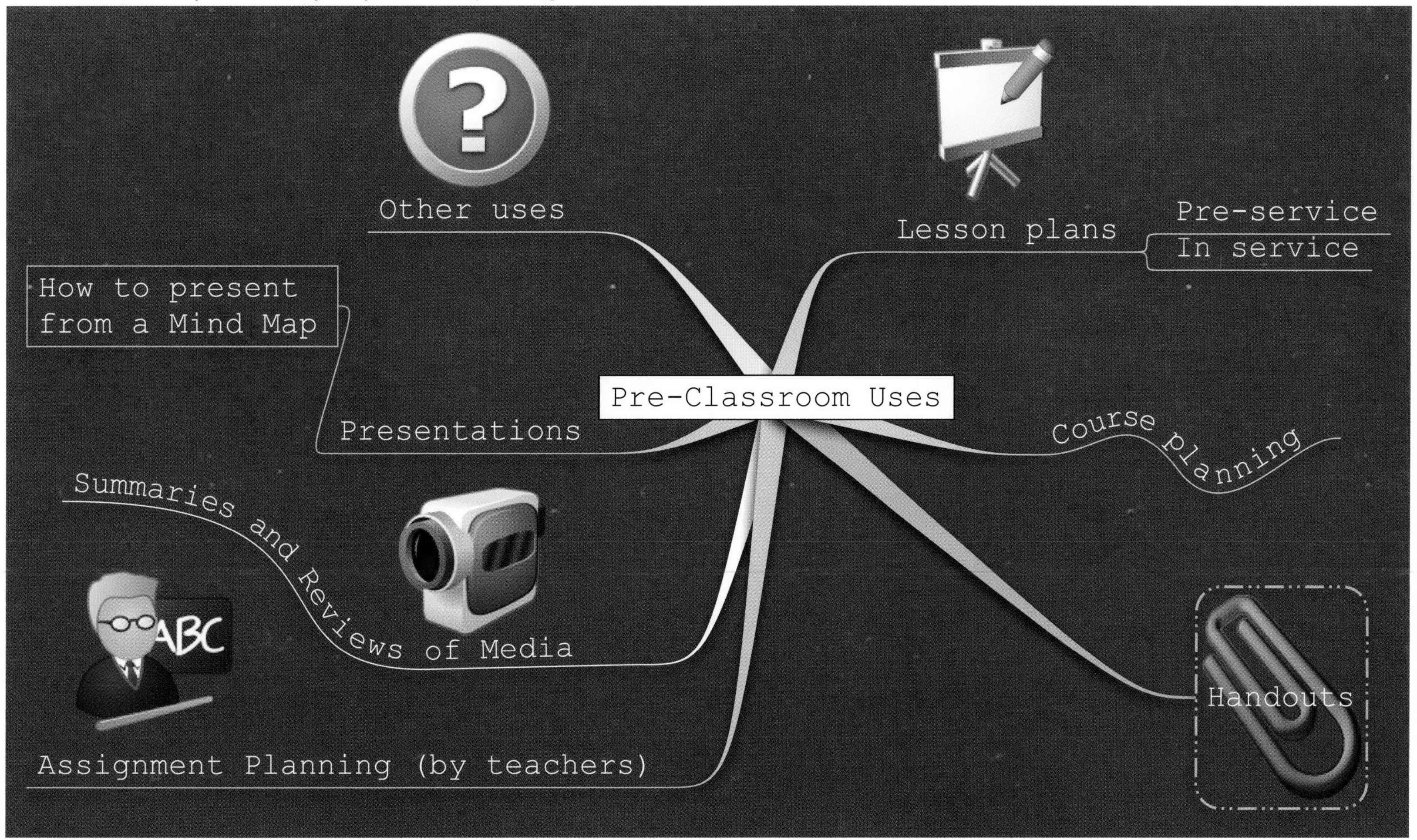

Lesson Plans

Pre-Service Teachers

The Mind Mapping process allowed the pre-service teachers to identify gaps in their knowledge which they could then either fill or work around.

Several research projects have been completed and many papers written about the benefits of Mind Mapping for pre-service teachers – both in their own learning and as they begin to move into classrooms.

A study of sixty-nine students in the third year of their Bachelor of Education (Primary/Elementary Teaching) Degree at the University of Wollongong[1] began by giving students tutorials in how to set up an electronic Mind Map. Over the course of three tutorials, the students were asked to use Mind Mapping to create a lesson plan for a subject of their choosing.

The pre-service teachers involved in the study spent considerable time outside of the set tutorials working on their Mind Maps and at the end of the study were enthusiastic about using Mind Maps on an ongoing basis.

The study participants found the Mind Mapping exercise useful on several levels. Firstly, it tested their knowledge of the subject they were planning to teach by requiring them to link together the knowledge they had. The researchers report that most of the students came to the tutorial sessions with lots of their own research material. In this way, the Mind Mapping process allowed the pre-service teachers to identify gaps in their knowledge which they could then either fill or work around.

Teachers were able to break down their subject into more manageable sections.

Secondly, by using Mind Mapping, pre-service teachers were able to break down their subject into more manageable sections – in some cases, such as the pre-service teacher who's subject was astronomy, they found that they were trying to encompass too large a subject matter in too short a time and so were able to quickly see that focusing on one specific area ('our solar system' as opposed to 'the entire universe') would be much more manageable and advantageous.

"Further, it appears many pre-service teachers did not realize how inadequate their understanding of the

1 *Brian Ferry, John Hedberg and Barry Harper, University of Wollongong, "How do Preservice Teachers use Concept Maps to Organize Their Curriculum Content Knowledge?", 1997 ASCILITE Conference, http://www.ascilite.org.au/conferences/perth97/papers/Ferry/Ferry.html*

subject matter knowledge was until they began to create concept maps. Often they had superficial knowledge of a few key concepts, but had little or no in-depth understanding of related concepts and how they linked together. It is likely that this would have impacted upon their ability to effectively instruct young children."

One of the main findings of the study was that pre-service students benefited from instruction on creating Mind Maps – both in the tutorial sessions and by using the electronic tutorials included with the software program.

The study also found that students saw the benefit in using a software program, versus trying to compile Mind Maps physically. As one of the participants said:

> *"I actually used pen and paper to try and prepare to come into the computer lab., but it was no use because I decided to re-design my concept map as soon as I started. The whole layout was different and the names changed. If I had used paper I would have to completely re-draw it. Also to have notes attached to concepts I found that I had to have a piece of paper attached to this concept and another to another concept and others attached to the links. Whereas if you're actually doing it as you are at the computer you haven't got all of these bits and pieces of paper all over the place....The tool keeps it nice and neat and you know where the notes are and can see them at any time when you want to check back."*[2]

Another study was conducted by Mohan Chinnappan of the University of Wollongong, focusing on pre-service teachers using Mind Mapping to further their understanding and thus their teaching ability, of mathematics.[3] It involved 30 pre-service teachers who were enrolled in the third year of their BEd (Primary) program.

Chinnappan maintains that one of the major influences in a child's ability to learn and understand mathematics is the understanding that their teacher maintains. He also states that an important part of a pre-service teacher's professional development is to construct links between what they know and how to teach it. This is very important in order to make the required knowledge easily understood by the primary students that these teachers will be teaching, but it becomes even more critical for secondary and tertiary educators who often have advanced degrees and specialist knowledge, and need effective methods to represent that information to

2 *Brian Ferry, John Hedberg and Barry Harper, University of Wollongong, "How do Preservice Teachers use Concept Maps to Organize Their Curriculum Content Knowledge?", 1997 ASCILITE Conference, http://www.ascilite.org.au/conferences/perth97/papers/Ferry/Ferry.html*

3 *Mohan Chinnappan, "Mathematics learning forum: Role of ICT in the construction of pre-service teachers' content knowledge schema", Australian Journal of Educational Technology, 2003, 19(2), 176-191. AJET 19*

their students. I experienced this personally at school where I was taught by teachers who had doctorates in their specialist subjects, but were not able to effectively communicate the information to the students. Using Mind Maps bridges the communication gaps at all levels, reducing frustrations for both the teacher and the students, as well as significantly increasing the information transfer.

By using Mind Maps to set out and draw links between the information they already possess, pre-service teachers can get an overall picture of where they stand, what gaps exist in *their* knowledge and how they can go about instructing their students in the most appropriate manner.

In this study, participants were split into five groups. Each of these groups participated in a series of online discussions in regards to teaching methods for K-6 mathematics.

Each of the group's discussions were then sorted through for useful content and that content was then transcribed into a Mind Map.

The Mind Maps produced allowed the researchers and the groups to see the content of the discussions and to interpret the underlying knowledge schemas. As a result of production and analysis of these Mind Maps, the researcher identified gaps in the understanding of the pre-service teachers in the study in relation to teaching K-6 mathematics (particularly in relation to multiplication).

Using Mind Maps bridges the communication gaps at all levels, reducing frustrations for both the teacher and the students, as well as significantly increasing the information transfer.

Lesson Planning – In Service Teachers

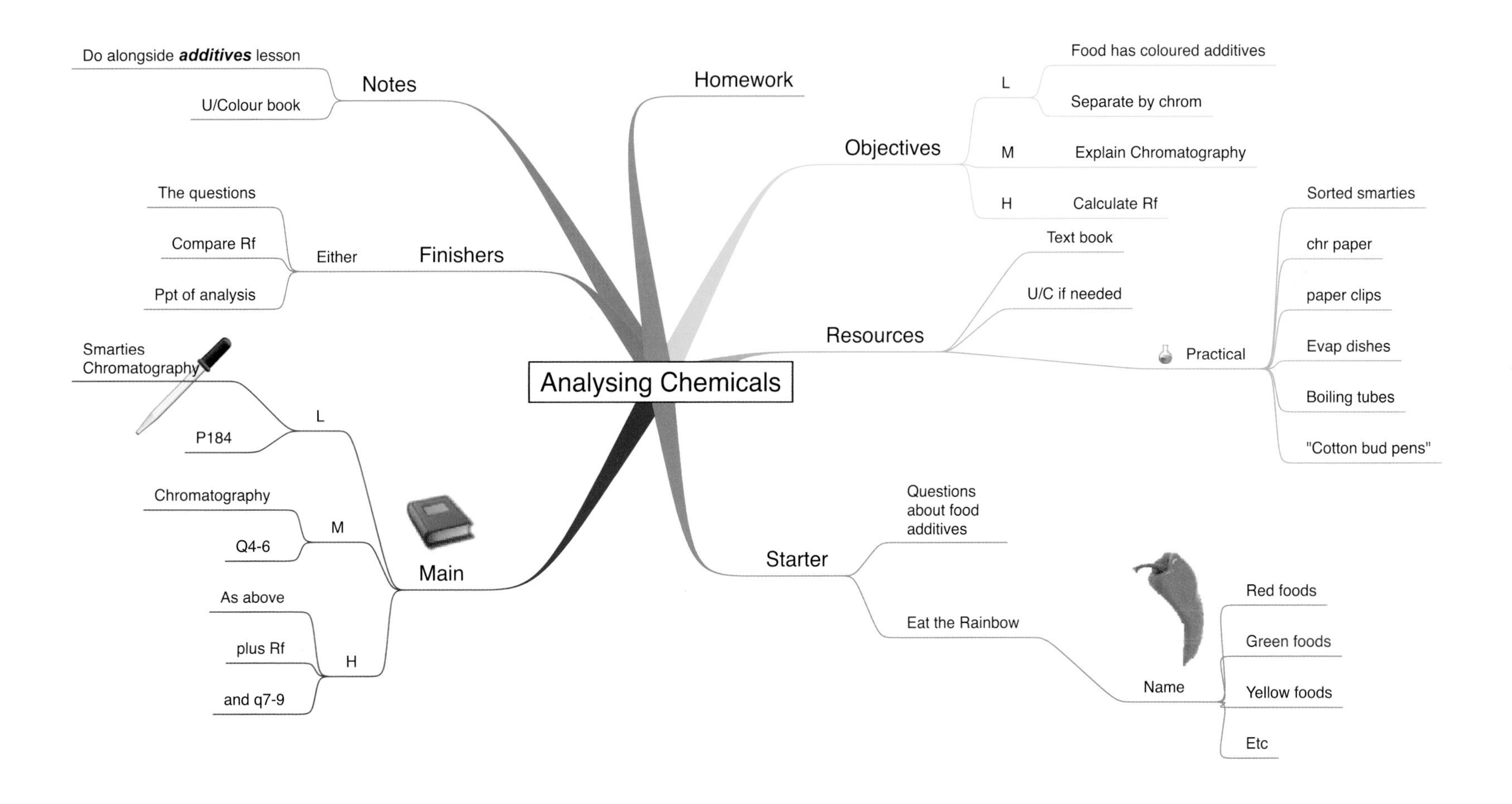

The Mind Map on the previous page, provided by Mark Gilchrist, a science teacher at Belle Vue Girls' School in the United Kingdom, shows how one teacher uses Mind Mapping as a Lesson Planning tool.

Mark says that when using Mind Mapping for Lesson Planning he goes through the following steps:

1. Look at (commercial) scheme of work;

2. Define objectives, main steps, resources and notes;

3. Map it out to act as an aid to my failing memory!

Mark also uses partially completed Mind Maps as handouts for his classes. To do this he follows these steps:

1. Identify the overall map;

2. Produce a starter map;

3. Project via PC and data projector;

4. Pen in other ideas;

5. Allow students to complete.

Many teachers follow the same (or a very similar) process, recognising that Mind Maps have many beneficial applications during lesson planning and delivery. As outlined above, pre-service teachers found Mind Maps invaluable as a resource for identifying the scope of the lesson plan and any gaps that may exist in their own knowledge.

In-service teachers find Mind Mapping their lesson plans valuable as they take far less time to compile than an ordinary lesson plan. The ability to cut and paste and hyperlink information from the internet and to hyperlink to Word documents make electronic Mind Maps particularly useful as a kind of resource database.

The ease with which these lesson plans can then be turned into handouts for classroom use (as outlined later in this chapter) makes them doubly effective.

An interesting experiment with an electronically Mind Mapped lesson plan would be to explore it's usefulness by joining an online Mind Mapping or education community and sharing the lesson plan with teachers throughout the world, seeing what they can add to it. An opportunity to join just such a group is presented at the end of this book.

Electronic Mind Maps truly excel in an online brainstorming arena, due to their ease of use and updatability.

As you become more comfortable with the Mind Mapping process, you will no doubt find many other ways to couple it with your lesson planning process.

Margaret Rees works with Wilderness Alert in Vancouver, Canada.

She has turned an entire 250 page Instructor Handbook into a series of Mind Maps, an example of which is shown to the right.

As you can see, Mind Maps can be used to good effect as an aid to preparing and presenting a course of this type. By outlining each area to be covered, the Mind Map makes it easy for the instructor to ensure that all vital areas of training are covered.

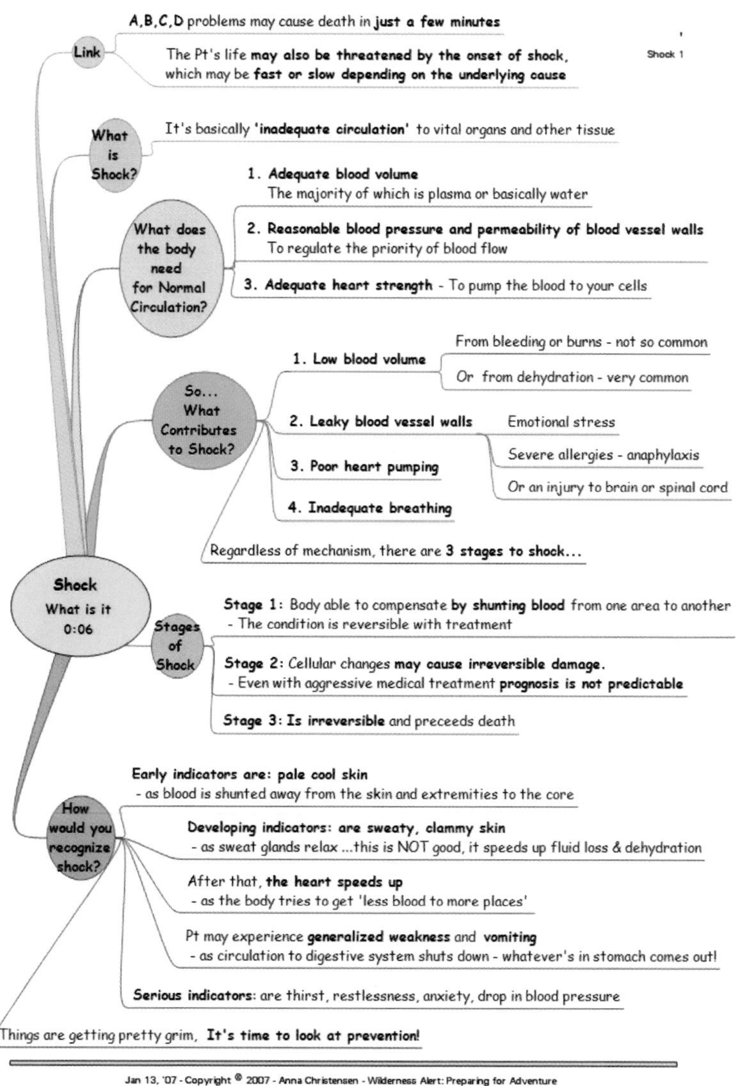

Course Planning

Mind Mapping is also well put to the use of planning out your entire course. It can help you look at particular goals you want to achieve with your students and then to look at the way in which the modules you are teaching lead in to this overall goal. It can help you identify gaps that may not have been obvious when thinking or noting these things in a linear manner.

Self-proclaimed Mind Mapping evangelist, Hazel Wagner, teaches business seminars. She says, "I teach adults, in seminar and workshop formats, mostly. I also teach at universities in business schools from time to time. I don't use 'lesson plans' like I did when I taught high school and junior high but the planning serves the same purpose."

Her method for this kind of planning is as follows:

1. Define Subject;

2. Brainstorm ideas around the main subject;

3. Print off Mind Map for handing out to students.

> *"I like to leave plenty of white space so students can write their notes right on the Mind Map. It gives them practice with Mind Mapping and proves the value of taking notes in that form."*

Mind Mapping can also be used for more extensive planning – term, semester or even year-long courses can be easily Mapped out on a single page, giving you an overview of how the course fits together. This can be a good subject orientation handout, allowing your students to see what will be taught to them and expected of them throughout the course.

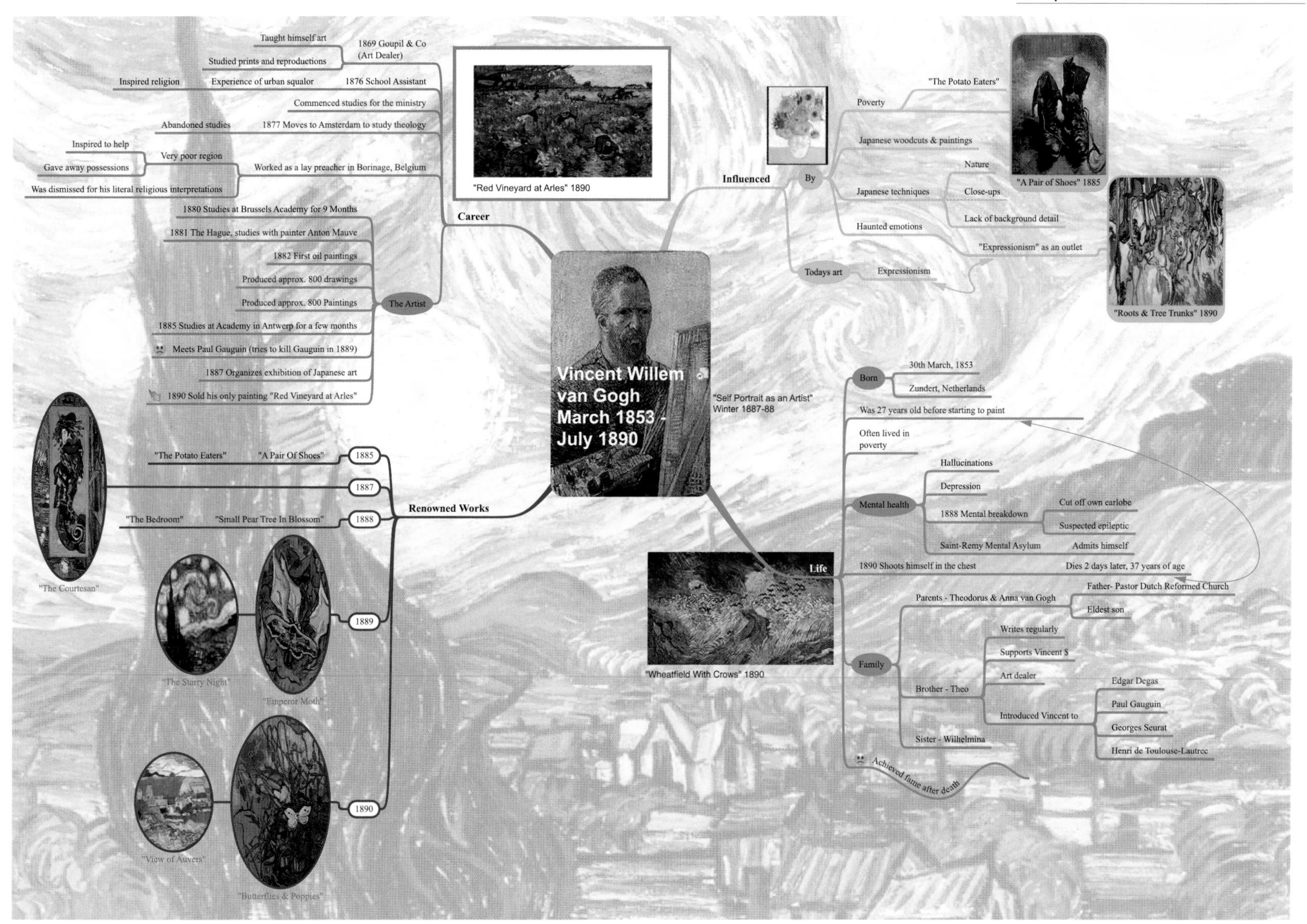
Vincent Willem van Gogh March 1853 - July 1890
"Self Portrait as an Artist" Winter 1887-88
Career
1869 Goupil & Co (Art Dealer)
Taught himself art
Studied prints and reproductions
1876 School Assistant
Experience of urban squalor
Inspired religion
Commenced studies for the ministry
1877 Moves to Amsterdam to study theology
Abandoned studies
Worked as a lay preacher in Borinage, Belgium
Very poor region
Inspired to help
Gave away possessions
Was dismissed for his literal religious interpretations
The Artist
1880 Studies at Brussels Academy for 9 Months
1881 The Hague, studies with painter Anton Mauve
1882 First oil paintings
Produced approx. 800 drawings
Produced approx. 800 Paintings
1885 Studies at Academy in Antwerp for a few months
Meets Paul Gauguin (tries to kill Gauguin in 1889)
1887 Organizes exhibition of Japanese art
1890 Sold his only painting "Red Vineyard at Arles"
"Red Vineyard at Arles" 1890
Influenced
By
Poverty
"The Potato Eaters"
Japanese woodcuts & paintings
Japanese techniques
Nature
Close-ups
Lack of background detail
Haunted emotions
"Expressionism" as an outlet
Todays art
Expressionism
"A Pair of Shoes" 1885
"Roots & Tree Trunks" 1890
Renowned Works
1885
"The Potato Eaters"
"A Pair Of Shoes"
1887
1888
"The Bedroom"
"Small Pear Tree In Blossom"
1889
1890
"The Courtesan"
"The Starry Night"
"Emperor Moth"
"View of Auvers"
"Butterflies & Poppies"
Life
Born
30th March, 1853
Zundert, Netherlands
Was 27 years old before starting to paint
Often lived in poverty
Mental health
Hallucinations
Depression
1888 Mental breakdown
Cut off own earlobe
Suspected epileptic
Saint-Remy Mental Asylum
Admits himself
1890 Shoots himself in the chest
Dies 2 days later, 37 years of age
Family
Parents - Theodorus & Anna van Gogh
Father- Pastor Dutch Reformed Church
Eldest son
Brother - Theo
Writes regularly
Supports Vincent $
Art dealer
Introduced Vincent to
Edgar Degas
Paul Gauguin
Georges Seurat
Henri de Toulouse-Lautrec
Sister - Wilhelmina
Achieved fame after death
"Wheatfield With Crows" 1890

Handouts

The Mind Map on the previous page, which documents the life of Vincent Van Gogh, could easily be a Lesson Map. The teacher could then distribute it as a handout – either as is, or perhaps with some of the information missing (as the example on the previous page shows) so that students can fill it in as they work through the information, thereby making the learning process more interactive.

You can see that in this example, most of the text has been removed from the Map, leaving only the essential signposts and a few titles.

The arrows linking information together have also been removed, in order to allow students to make these connections themselves.

Maps like these engage students in the learning process by asking them to physically contribute to its design. It is a widely accepted fact that writing information down raises information retention rates – this, added to the colours and graphics of the Map, help students when it comes to exam and assignment preparation (this is discussed in further detail in Chapter 4).

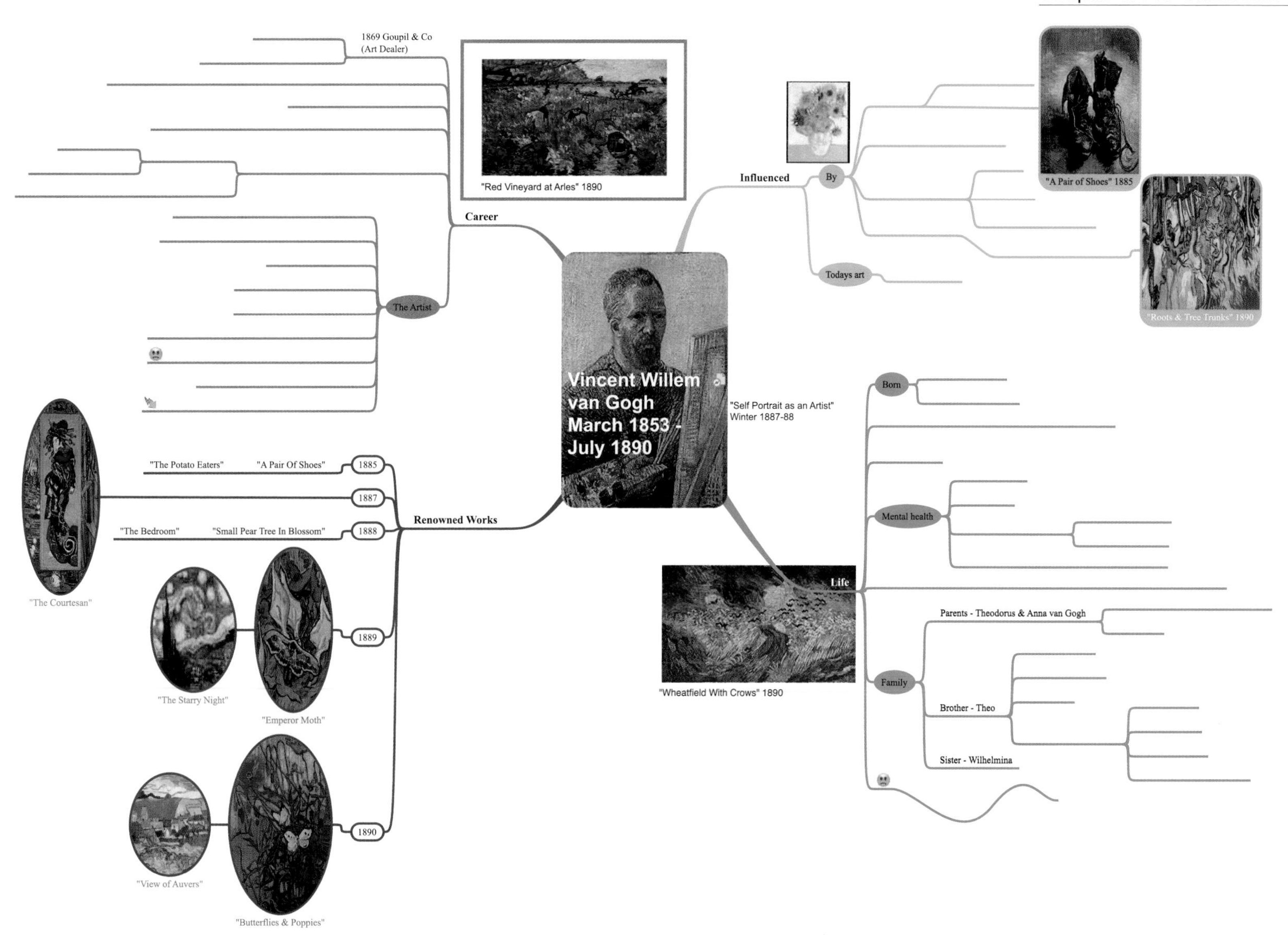
Vincent Willem van Gogh March 1853 - July 1890
"Self Portrait as an Artist" Winter 1887-88
Career
1869 Goupil & Co (Art Dealer)
"Red Vineyard at Arles" 1890
The Artist
Influenced
By
"A Pair of Shoes" 1885
"Roots & Tree Trunks" 1890
Todays art
Renowned Works
1885
"The Potato Eaters"
"A Pair Of Shoes"
1887
1888
"The Bedroom"
"Small Pear Tree In Blossom"
"The Courtesan"
1889
"The Starry Night"
"Emperor Moth"
1890
"View of Auvers"
"Butterflies & Poppies"
Life
"Wheatfield With Crows" 1890
Born
Mental health
Family
Parents - Theodorus & Anna van Gogh
Brother - Theo
Sister - Wilhelmina

Assignment Planning

Using a Mind Map as an assignment hand out will help your students keep track of precisely what it is you require from them.

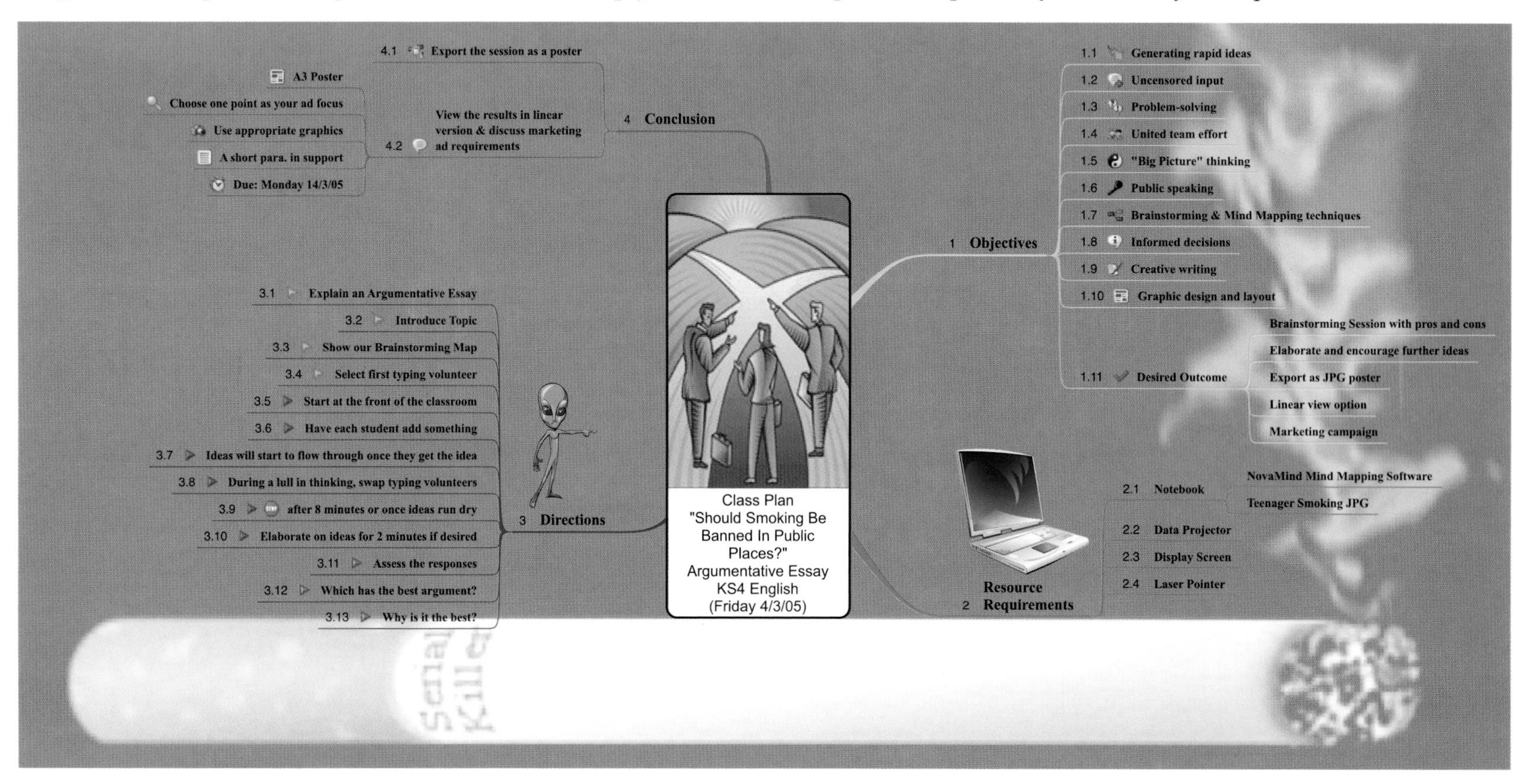

By placing the title of the assignment in the centre of the Map and having branches extending from it which capture the essential questions of the assignment, students are better able to fully grasp what is needed in order for them to pass.

Summaries and Reviews of Media

Summarising and reviewing media with a Mind Map is simple and the result can be used either purely for your own reference or, again, as a student handout.

Books, magazine articles and movies can all be Mind Mapped with excellent results.

Often these Maps will help students see themes within different works where they may have found it difficult from simply reading a book or watching a/ movie. By having them Map the story, themes and symbols within the work become self evident, allowing students to discover these for themselves.

Below is an example of a student Mind Map of the movie 'Remember the Titans':

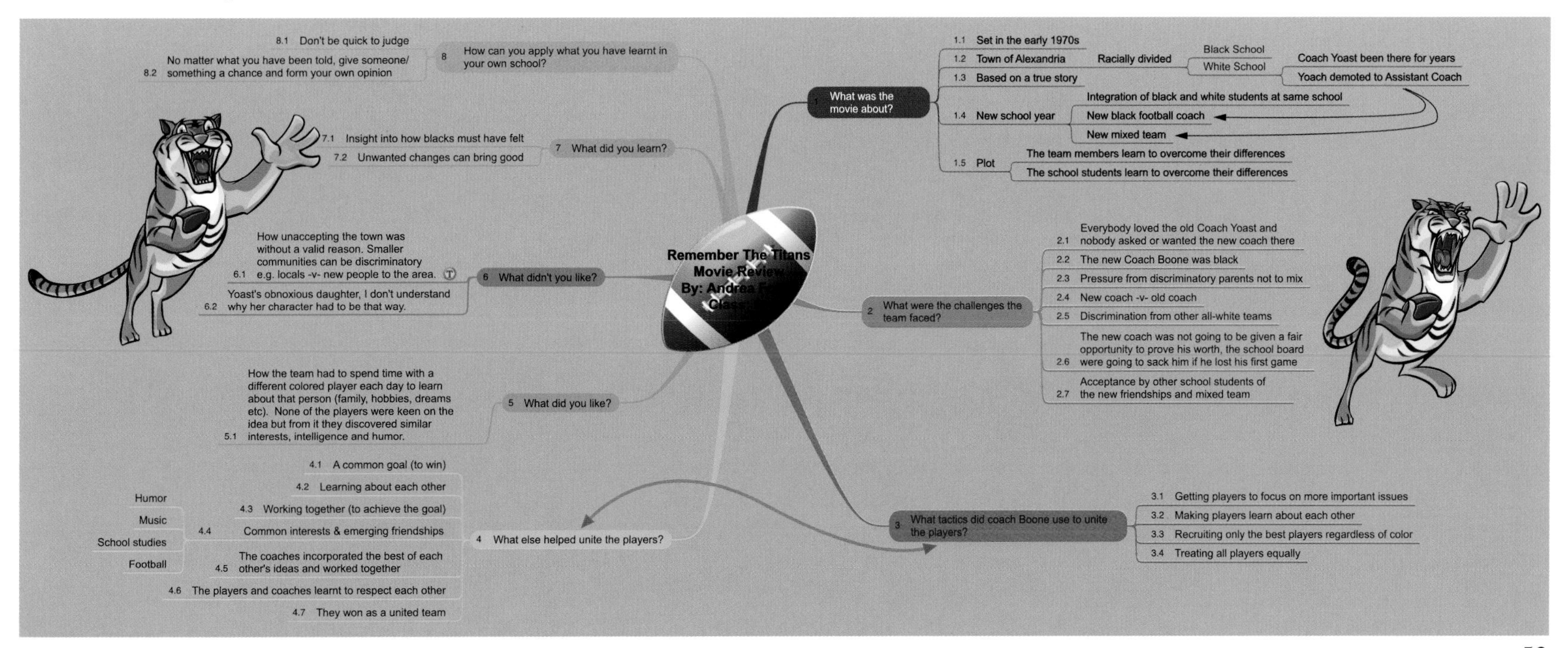

It is evident how useful this Map would then be to the student as a base for a written assignment analysing the movie, its themes and messages.

Presentations

To give a presentation from a Mind Map, you can:

- Print out the Mind Map to use as your notes; or
- Have the Mind Map on your laptop for you to see; or
- Project the Mind Map on a screen for all to see - perhaps using the Full Screen mode to make it easier (if your software has it).

Note that some Mind Mapping software allows you to print the Mind Map out without the text on the branches, as a handout. Why would you want to do this? Because this gives the opportunity for the following types of learning:

- **Visual** - as the students see the Mind Map on the screen;
- **Auditory** - as they hear you talking about it;
- **Kinestheticly** - as they write the text on the branches;
- **Creatively** - as they add their own branches to extend what you have written down in new ways using radiant, extensive thinking and creativity;
- **Personalised** - they can use their own words on the branches so that it has more meaning for them. They use the syntax they are most familiar with, understanding the semantics of the relationships between the ideas, and extending the Mind Map with their own thoughts as they go along.

The harnessing and building of these skills gives these students a massive learning advantage over others who are not using Mind Mapping.

When presenting from a Mind Map, make sure your presentation Mind Map is colourful and uses images where appropriate to add extra meaning to the image. If you can add humour through the images and words, all the better - it will be even more memorable.

If you are giving the presentation using a Mind Mapping software program and a projector, you can use the full screen mode to get the normal user interface out of the way. You might like to hide children branches until you get to them.

Some of the benefits of using a Mind Map in a presentation are:

- You always have the topic in front of you in the centre of your Mind Map, so you are less likely to go off on tangents. Or, if it is appropriate, it actually gives you the freedom to go off on a tangent, discuss this tangent thoroughly and easily return to where you were in your presentation, pre-tangent (imagine trying to do this with traditional presentation notes!);
- You have the main points in the first level branches, so when you go down to the detail levels, you are still conscious of the main point you are making;
- The whole presentation is there in one place - no more getting lost in your notes;
- There is a visual association through the branch lines and colours between related topics, adding clarity to your presentation;
- You can easily pace yourself through the presentation because you can always see how many things you have covered and how many more there yet to cover;
- If you are presenting using a projector and a Mind Mapping software program, you can hide the details and use progressive revelation to show the information, without your audience getting lost - they always know how the information fits in;
- You are working from appropriately summarised information which gives you clear visual cues as to where you are up to, so you can maintain better eye contact and rapport with your audience;
- You will be much better equipped to handle audience participation and feedback through the course of your presentation because

you have the confidence of the visual anchor to the current topic and a clear picture of what is coming up for the rest of the presentation;

- With the information organisation of a Mind Map, the information is being presented in the form that fits best with the way your brain operates, so the understanding and retention of the material is much enhanced and your presentations are smooth, clear and concise.

How to present from your Mind Map

To start your presentation, state what the topic is (from the Mind Map title), then go around the innermost branches to give an introduction and tell people what to expect from the presentation.

Next, go into the details of each of the branches in turn, stating the first level branch (main idea) before going into the detail and reiterating it at the end of that section.

At the end of your presentation, go back around the innermost branches to give a summary.

» *Stick to keywords on your Mind Maps, and let your speech flow from there.*

» *Think of your audience as your friends - they all want you to do your best.*

» *Keep an expanded awareness of the state of the listeners in the room.*

» *Tell stories - start early in your presentation, but don't finish the stories until right at the end - this will keep people interested in the whole presentation.*

» *Have your projections and visual aids to the left side from the audience perspective - they will remember it better there.*

» *Think what emotional states you want people in at different stages of your presentation, and design your content and presentation style to invoke those states in your audience.*

» *Remember that you will have people who learn differently in your audience - make sure you cater for:*

1. ***Visual learners*** *- by showing them things, and allowing them to "see" the "clear" benefits which they can "picture" and "imagine". You are in a position to "show" them the way things are so they can "watch" and "see" the results.*

2. ***Auditory learners*** *- by telling them things that they can "tune in" to, "harmonize" with and "listen to". Check in to see that you say "rings true" and "sounds good" to them. Make your message "clear as a bell", and ask them to "hear you out" and "listen to this".*

3. ***Kinesthetic learners*** *- by allowing them to "grasp" the ideas and really "come to grips" with your message. You can "lay all the cards on the table" so they can "get the drift" of what you are saying.*

» *Make sure you structure your presentation so that you cover the areas of:*

1. *Why they need to know this information.*
2. *What the information is*
3. *How it all works*
4. *What if the situation changes, or certain things happen etc.*

» *Keep questions until you get to the "What if" section of the presentation to make sure the message is covered and there are no interruptions to the flow, but also so that people know that there is going to be an opportunity for them to get their questions answered.*

Other Uses

There are a wide variety of other potential uses of Mind Maps. They could, for instance, be used as a planning tool for fieldwork – from organising the logistics of the outing through to a guide for students on how the outing relates to their course work.

If you are already using Mind Mapping or if you begin after reading this book and you use these Maps pre-classroom in ways not outlined in this chapter, please feel free to contact the author with details that may be included in future editions of this book.

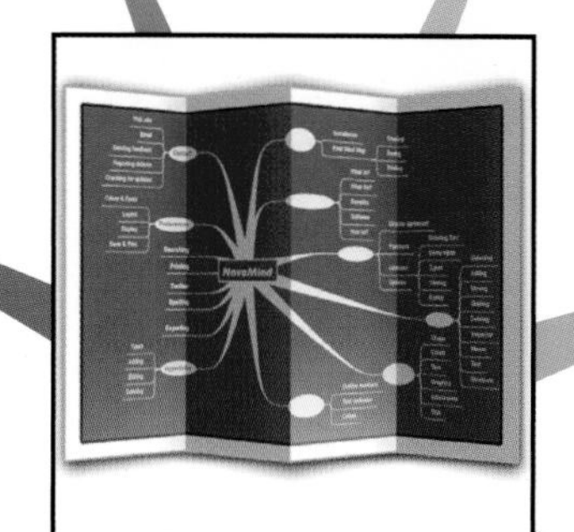

Chapter 3:
Pre-Classroom uses of Mind Mapping

Chapter 4: Mind Mapping in the classroom

In this chapter we will examine some case studies of Mind Mapping as used in classrooms and talk about various uses so you can see how this fits with your lesson planning and delivery, and student interactions in a practical sense.

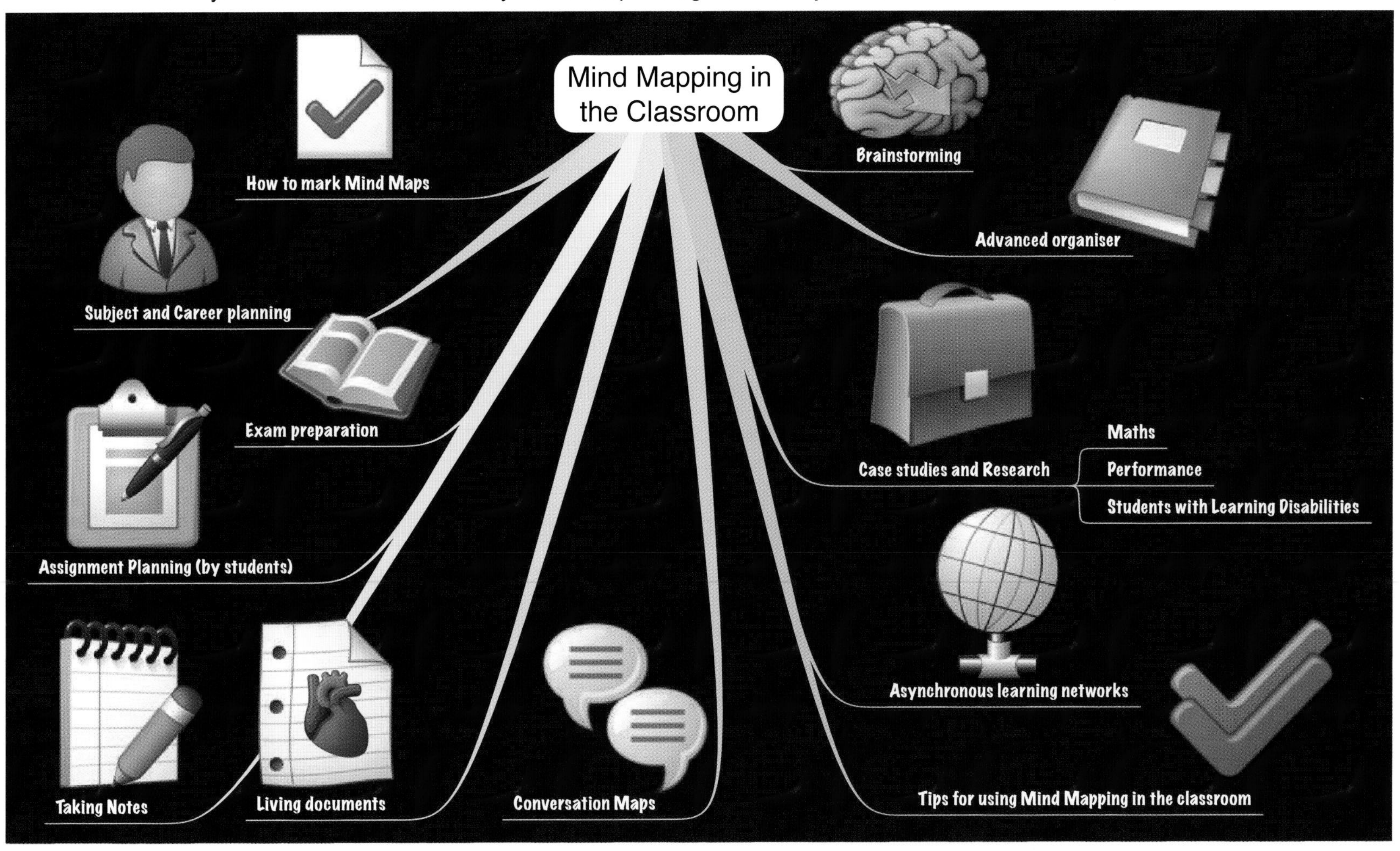

Brainstorming

Brainstorming is a creativity technique in which ideas are generated in order to solve a problem. The main result of a brainstorm session is a solution to a problem. The solution can be an idea, which is a complete solution to the problem. It can be a list of ideas, leading to an approach to a subsequent solution of the problem. Or it can be a list of ideas resulting into a plan to find the final answer. Brainstorming was originated by Alex Osborn.

Mind Mapping is particularly useful in a brainstorming capacity as, whether you are brainstorming on your own or in a group situation, it allows you to quickly and easily capture information. If the brainstorming session goes off on a tangent, you can also capture that and graphically and easily represent how the conversation got there and what the outcomes were – sometimes the diversions can be very useful in generating solutions or coming up with new ideas, whether they be for the issue at hand, or for other topics.

Brainstorming has many applications but it is most frequently used in:

- **Problem solving** - issues, root causes, alternative solutions, impact analysis, evaluation;
- **Project Management** – in terms of your students, this may mean managing their assignments and identifying objectives, risks, deliverables, resources, roles and responsibilities, tasks and issues;
- **Team building** - generates sharing and discussion of ideas while stimulating students to think;
- **Individual ideation**: by means of generating a maximum number of potentially usable ideas in a minimum of time;
- **Creative training**: brainstorming improves the creative attitude towards solving problems and improves the creative ability of your students, both in groups and individually. Although the main purpose of brainstorming is to generate ideas, a group brainstorming session has more value in problem solving;
- **Improve initiative**: during a brainstorm session, students are encouraged to constantly throw in their ideas, to take initiative all the time. This initiative can improve students' confidence and last even after the session;

- **Improve creative thinking**: students are encouraged to look at the problem from a creative perspective and the power of association is used to create ideas;
- **Improve morale**: the students work together as a team to find a solution to a problem and each of them is encouraged to take initiative. These two factors can improve the morale within the classroom and encourage an inclusive, rather than exclusive, environment;
- **Have more FUN**: most of your students will love the interactive and creative atmosphere in which problems are solved. In fact, they'll probably think that they've managed to trick you out of making them do 'real' work!

Approach

Brainstorming can be done either **individually** or in a **group**. In group brainstorming sessions, students are encouraged to share their ideas with one another as soon as they are generated.

The key to brainstorming is not to interrupt the thought process. As ideas come to the mind, they are captured and stimulate the development of better ideas.

You can break the class up into smaller groups or have them work as one large group. From a Mind Mapping perspective, depending on the age group of your students, you may wish to set up computers running a Mind Mapping software program or have students create their own Mind Maps by hand – either from a template or from their general knowledge of Mind Map construction.

In order to enhance creativity a brainstorm session has four basic rules:

1. Focus on quantity

This rule is a means of enhancing divergent production, aiming to facilitate problem solving through the maxim "quantity breeds quality". The greater the number of ideas generated, the greater the chance of hitting upon solutions.

2. Criticism is forbidden

In a group, it is often emphasised in brainstorming sessions that you should put criticism 'on hold'. When suspending judgment, you create a supportive atmosphere where participants feel free to generate unusual ideas.

This is particularly important in a classroom environment where students know one another and often certain students are more confident and outspoken than others. Removing the fear of criticism can build the confidence of the quieter students within the class.

3. Unusual ideas are welcome

By looking at things from another perspective, or by setting aside assumptions, some unusual ideas can be generated. These ideas will open new ways of working or thinking. It is easier to tame down an idea then to think up another completely new idea.

4. Combine and improve ideas

The approach of combining and improving ideas leads to better and more complete ideas and will cause a chain reaction of idea generation by using the power of association.

By introducing Mind Mapping via brainstorming in the classroom, you introduce your students to two very useful and important skills that will assist them throughout their studies and career.

Advanced Organisers

Mind Mapping can be used as an advanced form of organiser. Its uses extend from personal organising through to group organising.

By introducing students to the theory of Mind Mapping, it is possible to help increase their motivation and understanding – particularly of how the information they are receiving fits together with what they already know. Educational theorist, David Ausubel, asserts that the most important factor that influences learning is the knowledge the student already has. He says that for meaningful, non-rote learning to occur, the student must be able to see how new ideas relate to their preexisting knowledge.

Barbara Stäuble from Curtin University of Technology, Sarawak Campus, conducted a research project in which students of a University level Physics class were asked to both create and use Mind Maps in order to help them with self-direction, motivation and understanding[1].

Mind Maps were used in several areas of the subject in order to encourage students to link the new ideas they were learning to the information they already had.

A Mind Map was presented at the start of each lecture, presenting the ideas that would be covered. Once the lecture was completed, students were asked to add to the Mind Map and to draw connections between the new information they had learned that day and information they had previously learned.

In tutorials, students were asked to create their own Mind Maps and to develop criteria on which these Maps would be marked. The students then critically evaluated the work of their peers.

Each student took home their Mind Map and reworked it based on the feedback they had received.

Students reported a much higher level of:

- ✔ *understanding about the subject*
- ✔ *understanding the expectations placed on them*
- ✔ *motivation*
- ✔ *self-direction*
- ✔ *satisfaction with the subject*
- ✔ *learning outcomes.*

The research experiment was very successful, with students reporting a much higher level – not only of understanding about the subject and the expectations placed on them, but also of motivation and self-direction. There was also an increase in the overall level of student's satisfaction with the subject and with their learning outcomes.

This study clearly shows that, when combined with other educational tools – such as group work and peer evaluations, advanced organisers have a powerfully positive effect not only on student knowledge but also on their self-confidence and satisfaction with learning.

1 *Stäuble, B. (2005), "Using concept maps to develop lifelong learning skills: A case study". In The Reflective Practitioner. Proceedings of the 14th Annual Teaching Learning Forum, 3-4 February 2005. Perth: Murdoch University. http://lsn.curtin.edu.au/tlf/tlf2005/refereed/stauble.html*

These kinds of experiences promote life-long learning by encouraging students to make a positive link between the gathering of knowledge and deep levels of understanding. Further, teaching students a skill like Mind Mapping will serve them well as they can apply it to any subject they study or any hurdle they face in life.

Maths

Current theories on teaching children mathematics suggest that the old fashioned rote learning techniques are not properly equipping children with vital mathematics skills.

In a paper by Mohan Chinnappan from the University of Wollongong entitled "Mathematics learning forum: Role of ICT in the construction of pre-service teachers' content knowledge schema"[2], Chinnappan discusses concepts of improving student teachers' training in this area. His theories, however, contain valuable ideas for teachers at all levels of their careers.

The concept of 'knowledge modelling', wherein student teachers use a visual model to externalise information, is an excellent example of how Mind Mapping can offer benefits to both teachers and their students (the use of Mind Mapping as a Professional Development Tool is discussed further in Chapter 6).

By having students construct their own knowledge model, teachers encourage students to form links between the theories they are learning and their preexisting knowledge.

> *"Having constructed a model for a concept, teachers could go further and consider exploration of that model. Model exploration could involve activities that help children gain insight into the many interwoven connections that may have been established among the relevant knowledge components of the model. Such an exploration could reveal the structure of schemas to the learner. In this way children can be expected to access higher levels of prior knowledge and attempt to integrate that knowledge with elements of the model that is being constructed. The modelling process could also contribute to the expansion of networks of*

2 *Chinnappan, M (2003), "Mathematics learning forum: Role of ICT in the construction of pre-service teachers' content knowledge schema", Australian Journal of Educational Technology, 19(2), 176-191. AJET 19*

schemas that are associated with mathematical concepts resulting in deeper understandings."

Once the knowledge model is completed, teachers may choose to explore the models with the students. Examination of their own models and those of their peers will help students to develop critical analysis skills, as well as skills in assimilation and incorporation of new concepts and ideas, seeing where they fit into their own knowledge model.

An example is the mathematical application of knowledge models:

> *"Two models of multiplication are repeated addition and area/rectangular array. These macro models are built on sub-models which in turn are built on schemas of multiples and factors, grouping, properties of multiplication (commutative, associative, distributive) and multiplication algorithms. Repeated addition shows, for example, that 7 x 5 is equivalent to 7 + 7 + 7 + 7 + 7. It is important for children to understand the relationship between addition and multiplication. That is, multiplying 7 by 5 is equivalent to adding seven fives together. Modelling should aim to help children discover that adding seven fives together will give them the same result as adding five sevens (commutativity). The use of rectangular arrays provides an alternative way to help children visualise multiplication, but this strategy should be grounded in symbol manipulation as well, i.e. writing out 7 + 7 + 7 + 7 + 7 and seeing that it is equal to 35. Equally, children should be able to establish links between the symbols and elements that are located in the cells of the array."*[3]

By applying a Mind Map to the problem 7 x 5, students can manipulate the information in a variety of ways, coming to the conclusion that 7 x 5 is the same as 7 + 7 + 7 + 7 + 7 via their own natural curiosity and through using visual representations that are meaningful to them.

A more advanced multiplication Mind Map (for the multiplication of two binomials) may look like this:

3 *Chinnappan, M (2003), "Mathematics learning forum: Role of ICT in the construction of pre-service teachers' content knowledge schema", Australian Journal of Educational Technology, 19(2), 176-191. AJET 19*

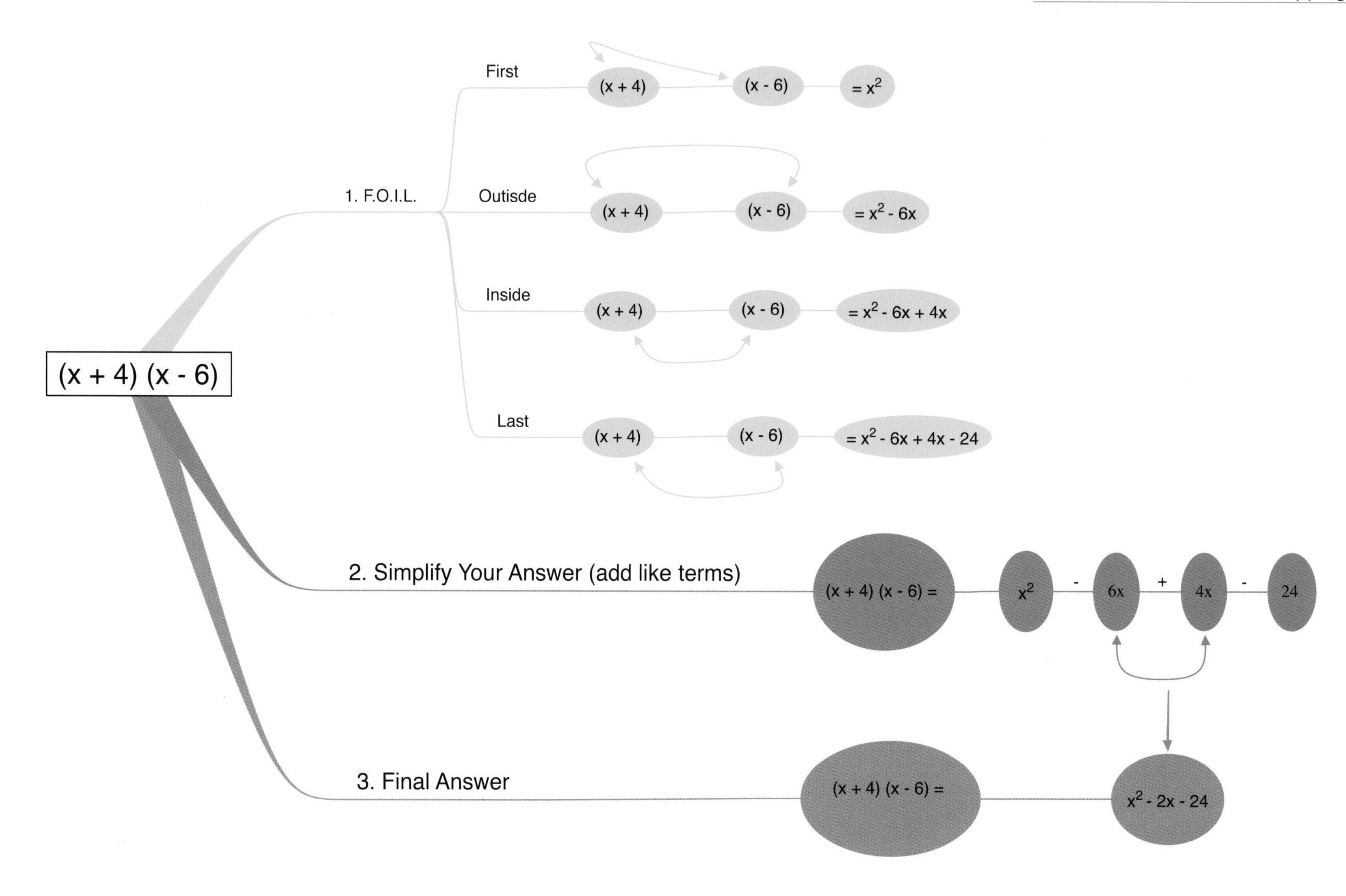

(x + 4) (x - 6)
1. F.O.I.L.
First
(x + 4)
(x - 6)
= x2
Outisde
(x + 4)
(x - 6)
= x2 - 6x
Inside
(x + 4)
(x - 6)
= x2 - 6x + 4x
Last
(x + 4)
(x - 6)
= x2 - 6x + 4x - 24
2. Simplify Your Answer (add like terms)
(x + 4) (x - 6) =
x2
-
6x
+
4x
-
24
3. Final Answer
(x + 4) (x - 6) =
x2 - 2x - 24

You can see from this Map that on the one page you can demonstrate to students all of the steps required to multiply two binomials.

When combined with the physical teaching of the subject, the Mind Map becomes an incredibly powerful illustration.

This is the perfect example of how Mind Mapping is not a replacement strategy for many of the classroom activities you currently conduct but can rather complement and enrich your teaching methods.

Where a student may have trouble remembering how to perform this operation from their own notes during a homework exercise, where they have a map like this, they have a clear, step-by-step map of what they need to do. By linking their thoughts back to the lesson with colours and an intuitive layout, the students recall and retention will be much greater than if they were trying to perform the task from their own notes or from a text book.

Helpless Handraisers

Mind Mapping can even be used as a class discipline tool, according to Dr. Fred Jones[4]:

> *"When you are presenting a lesson to the class, students tend to be relatively attentive. That's the easy part of the lesson. When you make the transition to Guided Practice and ask students to "work independently," the hard part begins. Typically, you're met with hands waving in the air -- the same hands every day; the same students saying the same thing: "I don't know what to do here." These are your helpless handraisers.*
>
> *If you tutor these students (typically 4-5 minutes), you reinforce helplessness, and while you are tutoring, you lose your mobility, which causes you to lose the entire class. In seconds, the noise level rises, which eventually forces you to do something.*
>
> *"Class! It is altogether too noisy in here. There is no excuse for all this talking when you have work to do. I cannot be everywhere at once..." You know the tune. It's no fun. There has to be a simpler way."*

4 *Jones, F (2006), "Dr. Fred Jones's Tools for Teaching Positive Discipline: Part 4: Visual Instruction Plans", Education World, http://www.educationworld.com/a_curr/columnists/jones/jones024.shtml*

Dr. Jones suggests that "Visual Instruction Plans" (Mind Maps) are an excellent way to show all of your "helpless handraisers" at once what to do and that the illustration will help them to understand with a minimum of input from you.

Performance

Craig Turner is an instructor at University of North Carolina at Chapel Hill, Department of Dramatic Art, Professional Actor Training Program. He conducts graduate courses in advanced movement training in a MFA three-year program, with admission by national audition, which trains performers for stage and screen.

"My work is in stage combat, juggling, movement analysis, mask training, Aikido, Taijiquan (a Chinese martial art - see attached Mind Map), stress mastery, performance state and process training through the body," says Craig.

Craig uses Mind Mapping to plan the semester / year for training and class sequencing, using the following method:

1. Define Subject: Movement Training for Actors;
2. Research Subject: Acting Process; Mind-body research; Trance-state performance; Mask; Stage Combat (all these and others, taking notes and incorporating into a sequence of training;
3. Collate Research and open Mind Mapping Program: I use DevonThink Pro to collect and categorize themes/ideas/topics and then export to my Mind Mapping program;
4. Brainstorm ideas around the main subject: This is something I do a lot of; Mind Mapping software lets me shift ideas and topics around, to see their relationship(s), and to make a coherent whole approach to a lesson/training sequence;
5. Analyse the subject: it's size and relevancy;
6. Using research, fill in any information gaps: Mind Mapping helps me see the gaps;
7. Print off Mind Map to hand out to students.

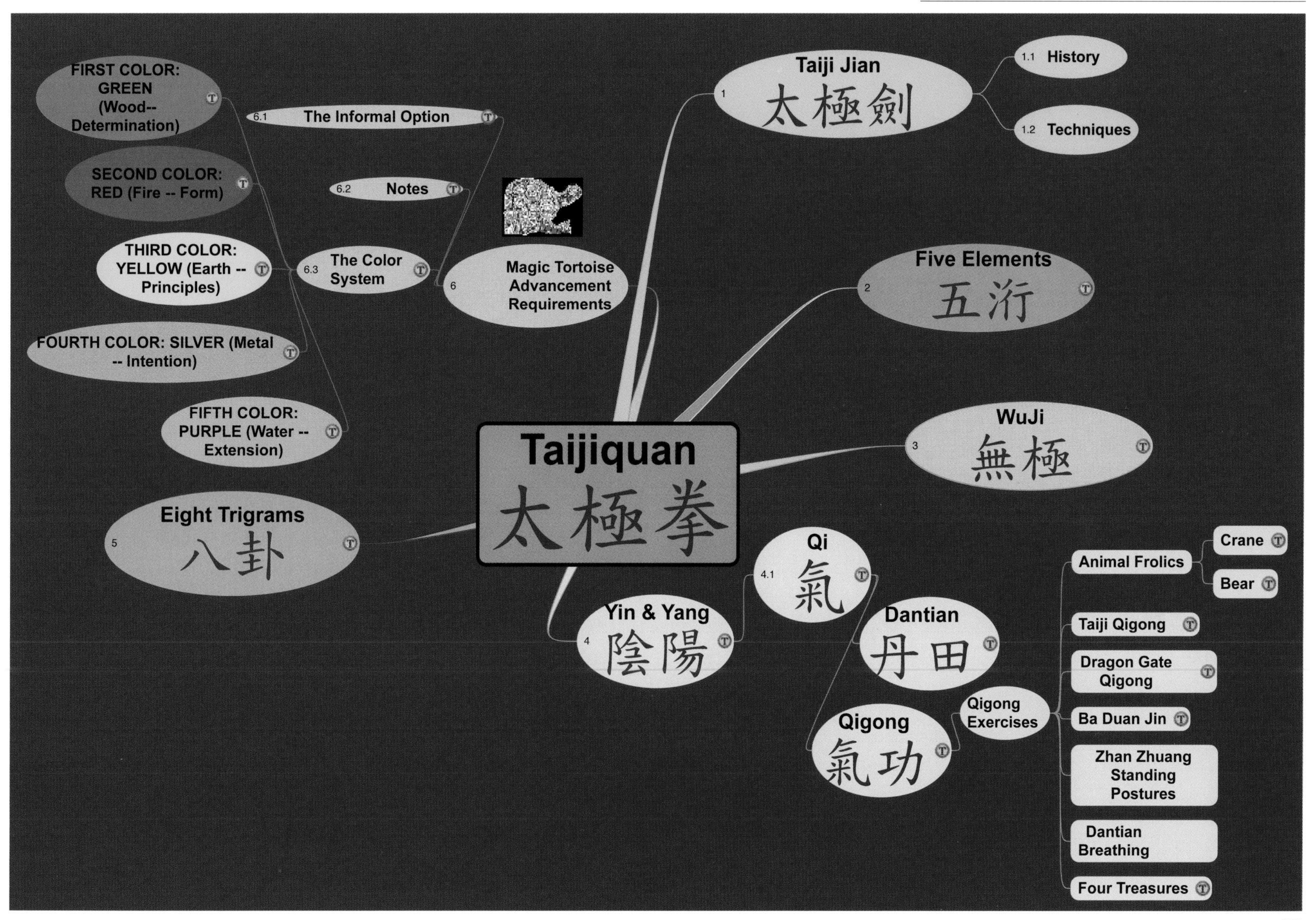

Taijiquan
太極拳
1 Taiji Jian
太極劍
1.1 History
1.2 Techniques
2 Five Elements
五行
3 WuJi
無極
4 Yin & Yang
陰陽
4.1 Qi
氣
Dantian
丹田
Qigong
氣功
Qigong Exercises
Animal Frolics
Crane
Bear
Taiji Qigong
Dragon Gate Qigong
Ba Duan Jin
Zhan Zhuang Standing Postures
Dantian Breathing
Four Treasures
5 Eight Trigrams
八卦
6 Magic Tortoise Advancement Requirements
6.1 The Informal Option
6.2 Notes
6.3 The Color System
FIRST COLOR: GREEN (Wood-- Determination)
SECOND COLOR: RED (Fire -- Form)
THIRD COLOR: YELLOW (Earth -- Principles)
FOURTH COLOR: SILVER (Metal -- Intention)
FIFTH COLOR: PURPLE (Water -- Extension)

Craig says:

> *"The most important thing I want to emphasise is how easy Mind Mapping makes it to see kinetic relationships within material. My mind is not frozen in time and my thinking is always provisional; there are many ways to train and teach. Mind Mapping helps me stay flexible as I seek out new approaches,"*

Using Mind Mapping with Students with Learning Disabilities

Studies showing that Mind Mapping increases the ability of students in areas such as reading comprehension, writing and high level thinking have particular relevance to students with learning disabilities.

The article "An Introduction to Concept Mapping Software"[5] on the Dyslexia.com web site notes that Mapping has been shown to have beneficial results in the following areas:

- ✔ vocabulary,
- ✔ writing,
- ✔ reading comprehension,
- ✔ high order thinking,
- ✔ comprehension and retention of scientific material and concepts,
- ✔ retention and recall of information along with time management,
- ✔ project planning,
- ✔ decision making.

The article notes that these are all areas that have been identified as particularly difficult for learners who have dyslexia, dyspraxia

5 *James, A (2006), "An introduction to Concept Mapping software", 26 July 2006, http://www.dyslexic.com/conceptintro*

or dyscalculia.

The article goes on to note that Mapping can be useful for structuring linear work, with ideas and concepts easily being rearranged and converted into a presentation or a linear document without the student having to consider sentence structure and grammar.

> *"Visual thinking is preferred by many people with dyslexia and seeing information graphically can increase both creativity and retention. Images can be used instead of words and features such as changing colours; re-sizing and spatial position can be used to convey information on topics, importance or actions to be taken."*[6]

The article also notes that other key benefits of Mapping for students with a learning disability include: the ability to store large amounts of information in a graphic format, making them easy to review and remember; and the graphical presentation of a problem, making it easier for students who have difficulties with literacy to grasp and thus solve.

I have had many emails from people who find Mind Mapping immensely helpful when dealing with ADD/ADHD, brain tumour/cancer recovery, brain injury recovery, and assisting people with brain development issues to learn. One such email I received was from Scott Wilcher, who said:

> *I can throw out all my ADD brain has in it and then focus on the branch I need to. The relationships become clear in my mind and the thoughts get untangled.*

Asynchronous Learning Networks

Asynchronous Learning Networks (or Distance Education Networks) are an ideal ground for Mind Mapping.

Mind Maps are a rich medium for communicating clearly in a Distance Learning environment. Using Mind Mapping software is particularly useful as the students can have hyperlinks to relevant material in the Mind Maps they are sent. They can also create Mind Maps that more clearly demonstrate their understanding of the topic better than they would be able to with traditional

6 *James, A (2006), "An introduction to Concept Mapping software", 26 July 2006, http://www.dyslexic.com/conceptintro*

methods. As the communication is only the message received rather than the message delivered, it is doubly important in the context of distance learning to have a clear representation of the student's understanding of the material, and Mind Maps provide an excellent way to ensure that the message delivery was effective.

The Maps could also be used in a 'live' capacity where the class engages in online group work – as a 'conversation map' or a 'live document' (for more information, see below).

Tips for Using Mind Maps in the classroom

The University of Minnesota's web site[7] contains the following information not only on why Mind Mapping is a useful exercise, but also on how the University's lecturers use Mind Mapping – as a class activity and as a planning and grading metric.

HOW TO: Approach Mind Mapping with your Students

> *"Before you decide to use mind mapping to teach, you should have a clear idea of your goals. Share them with your students when you assign the Mind Mapping activity and make sure you adequately introduce it:*

- Explain the benefits of using graphic tools in order to motivate students to try this technique;
- Explain the technique of mind mapping;
- Show them a mind map you've created and talk through the process;
- Discuss how you benefited from the process. Specifically, what does the mind map reveal or clarify?;
- Explain how you might use the mind map. For instance, if this is the first step in drafting a paper, how might you proceed to the next step? How might you use mind mapping to integrate and synthesize information, to study for an exam, or to generate a

7 *"Teach with Technology: Mind Mapping", University of Minnesota, http://dmc.umn.edu/activities/mindmap/*

thesis?;

- Explain how you will assess the students' maps."

Conversation Maps

Mind Maps make excellent conversation maps.

The difference between a regular Mind Map and a Conversation Map is merely that the Conversation Map is incomplete. It is filled in by the students as the conversation progresses (either literally – each student has their own Map, or figuratively – all of the students contribute to the one Map with the teacher or student representative filling in their ideas).

Conversation Maps are most appropriate in arenas where you wish to keep students particularly focused on the topic at hand. It allows the confirmation of current knowledge without allowing too much tangent in the conversation.

The benefits of Conversation Maps include: they direct a conversation without stifling ideas and creativity; they allow students to enter their own information, increasing their retention and recall rates; they use colours and graphics, also increasing information retention and recall; most of all - they are FUN! Students enjoy the interactive, group aspects of working with their peers to solve problems and come up with new ideas.

Living Documents

> *"A seminar differs from a lecture in that it lays more emphasis on process: in a more-or-less open-ended discussion among all members of the group, there is a less linear progression of ideas than there is in a lecture. A Map can be useful for keeping track of the flow of ideas in such a context, and for tying them*

together and commenting on them."[8]

A living document is slightly different from a conversation map, in that it may not be a group interaction activity.

A living document is more suitable in, say, an online university tutorial or distance education situation where the lecturer creates the map as they progress through the topic. Living documents allow total free form thinking, inspiration and creation. They begin with the topic in the centre of the Map, however, unlike Conversation Maps, the rest of the Map is created as the conversation progresses.

This sort of Map is most appropriate in an arena where, while the central theme is important, you wish to encourage students to really think for themselves – drawing their own conclusions and producing their own ideas on a certain topic or problem.

When conducting this type of lesson, it is a good idea for the tutor to have their own Mind Map of the directions they want to go and the important topics to cover already prepared, in order to gently direct the conversation where necessary and ensure that the important points are covered at some point along the way.

I have used Mind Maps in more traditional seminar settings where I was working from a Mind Map I had prepared and leading the discussion, and found it very helpful in conducting sessions where it was open for discussion, and where the topics sometimes were covered in a different order to what I had them in my Mind Map because that is the direction the audience wanted to go. It made it easy to go with the flow, make sure that that topic was covered completely, and that it was tied neatly back into the overall topic, and mentally (or sometimes physically) marking off the "blue branch" as having been covered.

This also means that in doing the summary at the end (as per the information given previously about giving presentations from Mind Maps), that topic was also covered. Also it made it easy for me to jot down notes during the presentation about some extensions or new ideas that I could feed back into the Mind Map for summary notes or future seminars.

Taking Notes

"Some people use Mapping to take lecture notes. If you find that this works for you, by all means do it:

8 *"Concept Mapping", http://www.coun.uvic.ca/learn/program/hndouts/map_ho.html*

however, if it does not work, you can certainly take lecture notes as you normally would, and summarize them later (as soon as possible after the lecture). Be sure to do this first from memory -- then check it over for accuracy. If possible, give yourself adequate time to do this -- the more time you spend, the better your retention will be. However, even a brief summary will have very beneficial effects for your memory, and your overall understanding of the material - its salient points and how they fit together."[9]

Encouraging students to use Mind Mapping to take notes is an investment in their future. The younger they begin using Mind Maps, the more benefits they will gain as they progress through their education.

A simple note taking Mind Mapping exercise (see Chapter 7 for specific details) can help students decide whether this is a method that will work for them.

As suggested in the quote above, another way to approach this is to have students take notes in a normal fashion and then to later transcribe them into a Mind Map.

It is important to allow students to decide for themselves which of these methods work better – to force them into taking notes with Mind Mapping when it doesn't suit their particular learning style would go against the entire philosophy of Mind Mapping!

Assignment Planning (by students)

The most valuable aspect of Mind Mapping in relation to planning anything, but particularly in relation to planning assignments, is that it can lay out a large amount of information in a compact format on one page, showing the associations between the different tasks and requirements.

Students can use Mind Mapping for four major areas of their assignments.

- Firstly, depending on the level of the students you teach, Mind Mapping may be appropriate for self-directed learning – such as for PhD students who are trying to make a decision on what to write their thesis about. As a brainstorming tool, Mind Mapping

9 *"Concept Mapping", http://www.coun.uvic.ca/learn/program/hndouts/map_ho.html*

is unparalleled. Students can set out all the different possible variations of their thesis topic and then follow these up by tracking how much they already know about the subject.

- Secondly, if you have not already provided them with a Mind Map of the assessment criteria, students should do this for themselves. This will ensure that they remember to address each of the criteria and will keep them focused and on track.
- Thirdly, students can use a Mind Map to physically set out their assignment.
- Finally, Mind Mapping is a very useful tool for organising information. Particularly when students are required to research vast amounts of material, Mind Mapping is very useful in helping them keep track of and sort out all of the information they have collected. This is particularly true when using Mind Mapping programs where you can have hyperlinks on the branches to open other documents and web pages with additional information on them.

Requiring students to submit their Mind Maps with their assignment is a good way of tracking not only the students' progress with the skill of Mind Mapping, but also the usefulness of using Mind Mapping techniques.

Exam Preparation

> *"Mapping can be a productive way to study for an exam, particularly if the emphasis of the course is on understanding and applying abstract, theoretical material, rather than on simply reproducing memorized information. Doing a Map of the course content can point out the most important concepts and principles, and allow you to see the ways in which they fit together. This may also help you to see your weak areas, and help you to focus your studying."* [10]

Using Mind Mapping during revision for exams can be incredibly beneficial for students.

Often, the sheer volume of information learned over the course can cause students to despair and feel overwhelmed when they come to revise.

10 *"Concept Mapping", http://www.coun.uvic.ca/learn/program/hndouts/map_ho.html*

Encourage students to begin their revision by making a Mind Map of the central concepts of the course. This will help them to recognise that there are a limited number of core ideas within the course and that each of those core ideas has a limited number of main details. By looking at the course in this way, students are less likely to be overwhelmed by what may otherwise seem like a never-ending deluge of information. Mind Mapping takes the complexities of thick text books and screeds of notes, and converts it into the minimalistic core semantics and basic keyword syntax that accurately and compactly embodies the subject material.

A Mind Map will also help students to identify the areas in which they feel comfortable and the areas in which they are not as strong and may need to concentrate their revision on. By recreating Mind Maps from memory during revision, they get the full benefit of all the learning modalities, making it quick and easy for them to understand and absorb the material.

Subject and Career Planning

For Senior High School students, subject and career planning can be one of the most stressful periods of their school careers.

Choosing the correct subjects so that they will be able to obtain the university place of their choice can be difficult and stressful for a person of any age – let alone a sixteen year old!

By introducing your students to Mind Mapping you can reduce some of that stress and more importantly, can help students to really think through their choices.

This has been a substantial problem in modern education – students are asked to make choices at a very young age about the rest of their lives, but are not always equipped with the resources, skills and information to make an informed and practical decision. Many, then, find themselves at the end of high school with some idea of where they want to go – but without the background subjects to make the move into the course.

There are now a number of programs that are addressing this issue. One, which has been put into place in Queensland (Australia) High Schools, is a Senior Education and Training (SET) program which has been introduced for Year 10 students. The program has students discuss their options with their parents and school and think about their strengths and interests and put all of these into a plan.

> *"The SET Plan lays out the subjects and courses the student needs to take to achieve his or her personal goals, as well as giving information on time management and study options, and back-up plans just in case some subjects or courses don't work out."*[11]

Clearly, Mind Mapping is a useful tool within the SET Plan. Students use it to brainstorm with their parents, teachers, peers and on their own, taking into account a range of different possible future careers and the paths they would need to take to get there.

This is a tool called *reverse engineering*, wherein you begin with the goal you want to reach and work backwards through each step that it will take to get there. Often, working backwards in this way, is easier for people than working out how to get to their goal from where they are now.

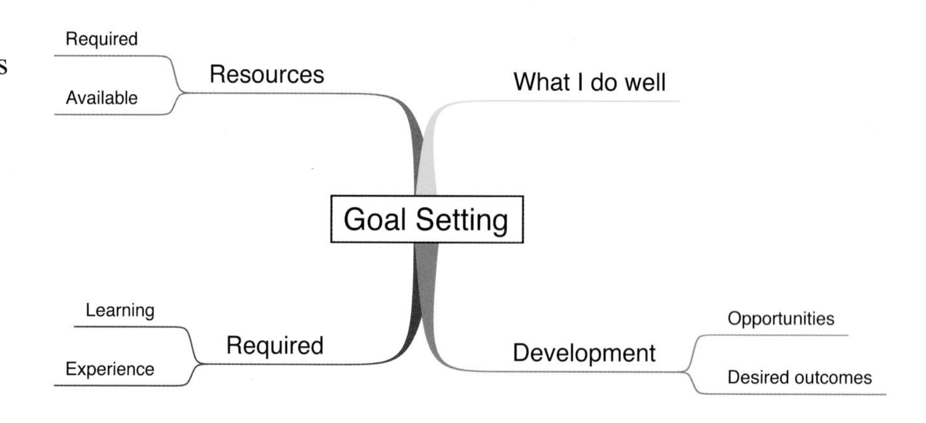

A Mind Map such as this one could be used as a starting point to help the student identify their strengths, areas that they want to develop and their desired achievements, and what they need to do to achieve those outcomes.

An example of a career goal Mind Map may look like the one on the opposite page.

As you can see, this Mind Map lays out for a student, on one page, their options for getting into the career they are interested in, the different paths they can take to get there and where those paths may eventually lead.

Now, they can look at whether they would prefer to study at TAFE (Technical and Further Education institution) or University, what kind of position they are looking at depending on which course they choose and what subjects they need to be looking at now to fulfil entry requirements.

---

11 *"Year 10s SET to plan for success", School + Parent Magazine, Issue 1, 2004, http://education.qld.gov.au/publication/reporting/parents/2004/issue1_year10.html*

Further, students could make separate Mind Maps for more than one possible career and then collate them onto a 'Mega Career Map', or hyperlink them off a master summary Mind Map. This would allow them to ensure that their subject selection kept a range of course and career options open to them.

Of course, for those who may be looking at going into vocational training, Mind Mapping can be just as useful – in the planning

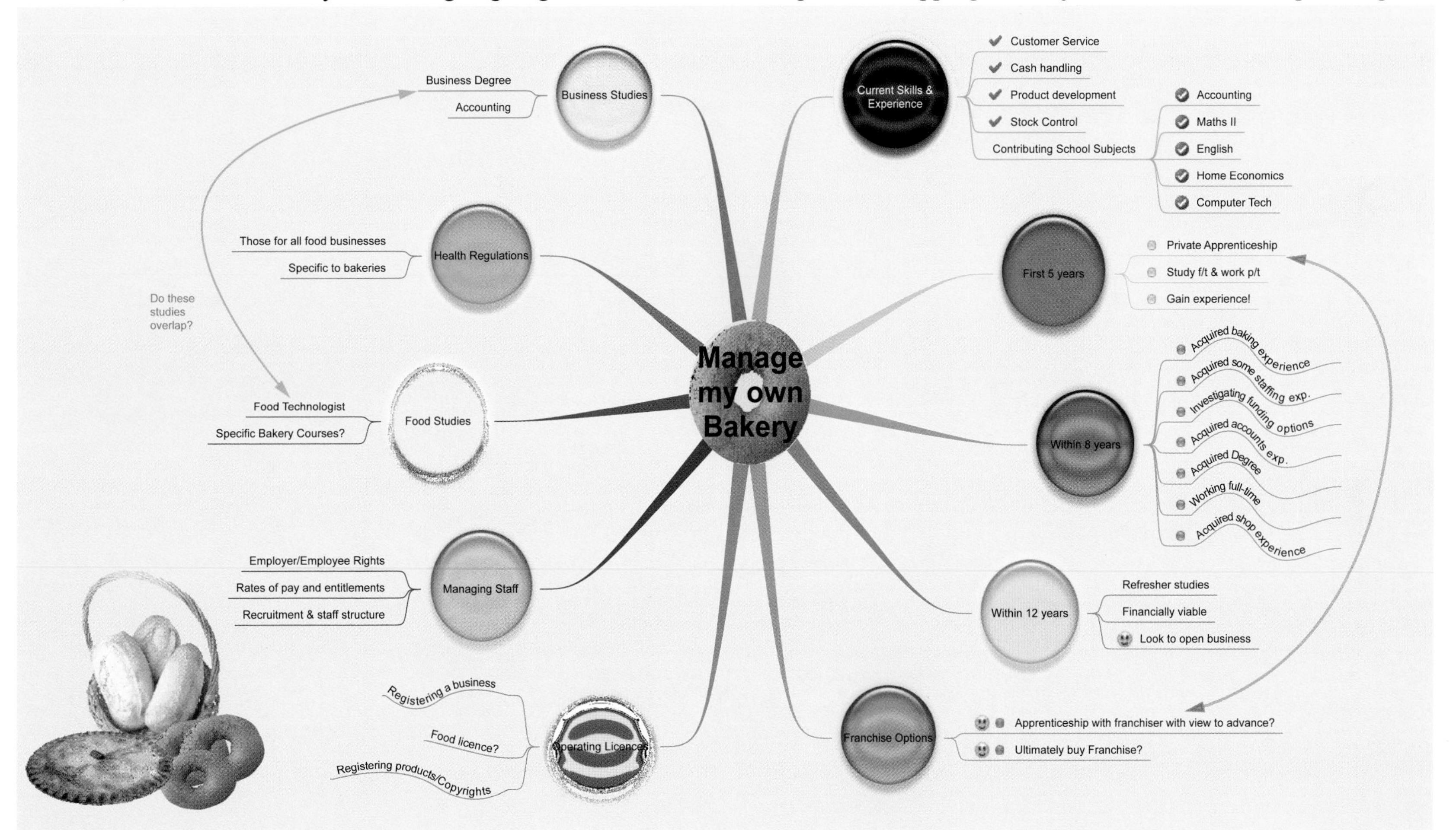

stages, during their study and throughout their careers. Many students who complete vocational training end up as small business owners – skills like Mind Mapping are, at that point, absolutely essential to their ability to run a successful business.

For more information on specific uses of Mind Maps in the classroom, see Chapter 7 for a variety of lesson plans and examples that could be incorporated into your classroom

Marking Mind Maps

If the wonderful thing about Mind Maps is their encouragement of creativity and intuitive and personal nature – how do you go about marking them?

The University of Minnesota's Digital Media Centre has kindly given us permission to reproduce these grading rubrics that their staff have developed and use.

MIND MAP (Total possible points 12)

- **Structure:** non-linear structure that provides a complete picture of your ideas **(3 points)**
- **Relationships:** relative importance of ideas is indicated and both simple and complex relationships are very effectively mapped **(3 points)**
- **Communication:** information is presented clearly and allows for a high level of understanding **(3 points)**
- **Exploratory:** map shows complex thinking about the meaningful relationships between ideas, themes, and the framework **(3 points)**

HRD 5103: PSYCHOLOGICAL FOUNDATION OF HRD

[HUMAN RESOURCE DEVELOPMENT]

Grading Rubric Assignment 1: Mind Map

Total possible points: 20

	Points	**Comments**
Mind Map		
Structure		
Relationships		
Communication		
Exploratory		
Text		
Communication		
Relationship with HRD		
Other		
Article chosen is relevant		
Assignment was completed on time		

TEXT (Total possible points 6)

- **Communication:** information is presented clearly and allows for a high level of understanding **(3 points)**
- **Relationship with HRD**: a clear link is made between the information in the article and the field of HRD **(3 points)**

OTHER (Total possible points 2)

- **Relevance of article:** article was of scholarly quality and relevant to psychology and HRD **(1 point)**
- Assignment was handed in on time **(1 point)**

Concept Map [Assessment Rubric]

Criteria	Excellent	Good	Adequate	Marginal	No credit; is Unacceptable to review
Structure	Non-linear structure that provides a very complete picture of your ideas	Non-linear structure that provides a complete picture of your ideas	Non-linear structure that provides a picture of your ideas	Non-linear structure that shows some relationships between ideas	Inappropriate structure
Relationships	Relative importance of ideas is indicated and both simple and complex relationships are very effectively mapped	Relative importance of ideas is indicated and relationships are very effectively mapped	Relative importance of ideas is indicated relationships are mapped	Importance is evident but not very distinctive; relations are somewhat clear but lacking	No differentiation between ideas; no evidence of meaningful Relationships
Exploratory	Map shows complex thinking about the meaningful relationships between ideas, themes, and the framework	Map shows effective thinking about the meaningful Relationships between ideas, themes, and the framework	Map shows definite thinking about Relationships between ideas, themes, and the framework	Map shows some thinking about Relationships between ideas, themes, and the framework	Thinking process is not clear
Communication	Information is presented clearly and allows for a high level of understanding	Information is presented clearly and allows for a good level of understanding	Information is presented clearly and allows for a basic level of understanding	Information is presented and some understanding can be gained	Information is not clear, very difficult to understand

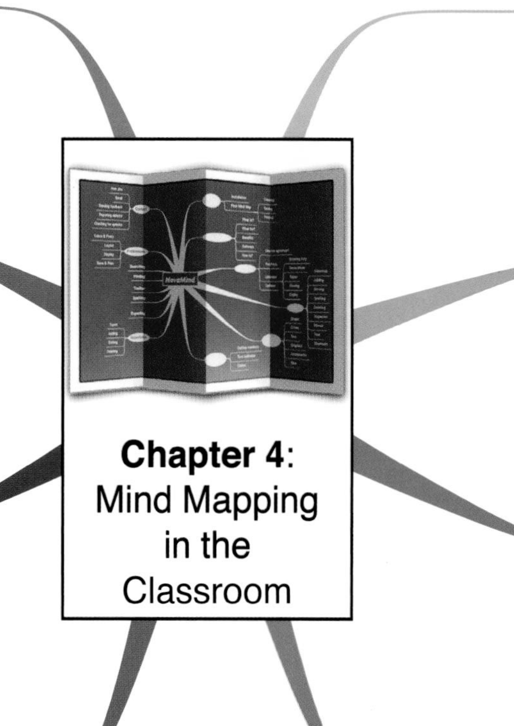

Chapter 4: Mind Mapping in the Classroom

Chapter 5: Constructing Mind Maps

In this chapter we will go into some of the practicalities of Mind Mapping, both individually and in groups; both by hand and using computer software.

We will also give some broad guidelines on choosing the right Mind Mapping software for your needs.

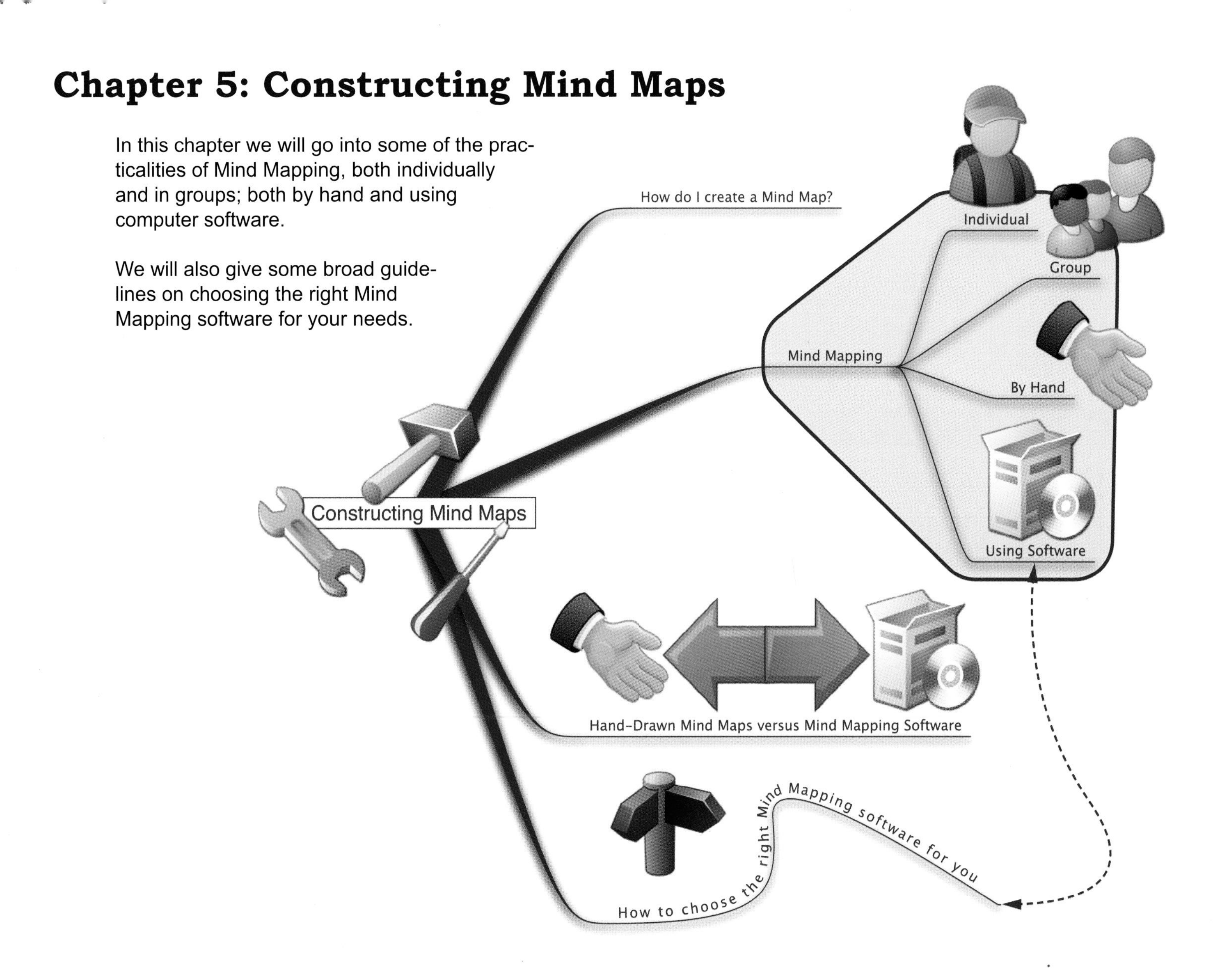

How do I create a Mind Map?

Given the intuitive nature of Mind Mapping, it is a fairly easy skill to learn. However, like any new skill, it takes practice to perfect.

There are two ways in which you can construct a Mind Map – the first is by hand, the second is via Mind Mapping software. Following are instructions on the creation of both, along with instructions for Mind Mapping in a group situation.

In Chapter 1, we included a Mind Map on "The Laws of Mind Mapping" - I suggest you go back and review that to see what works well. By this point in the book, you have also been exposed to a variety of different styles of Mind Map created by myself and others from all over the world.

The more you practice, regardless of whether you Map by hand or with software, the more you will find that Mind Mapping is not only intuitive, easy and fun, you'll also find it is an essential skill in your repertoire.

Mind Mapping by Hand

You will need:

- Large piece of paper – preferably, larger than A3
- Coloured pens / pencils / crayons
- Pictures from magazines

If you can, hang the piece of paper from the wall orientating it to Landscape (this gives you enough room to move through branches and add graphics). In the centre of the piece of paper write the subject / goal / intended outcome for your map– if you can, include a sketch (or paste a picture) that represents this.

Using different coloured pens, begin drawing branches from the central word or image – these branches should not be straight, but rather should curve and flow from the central image. These branches contain what are known as the Basic Ordering Ideas or BOIs. On each BOI branch use a single word or image to represent the main thoughts that relate to the central idea. If using words, be sure to use printed letters as they are easier to read, particularly at a glance.

Don't be overly critical of the ideas you come up with or the words you write. The Map is a reflection of your brain – whatever is going on in there should be put down on paper!

Now, begin looking at the next level. From each BOI draw a branch, or a series of branches and again add words or images that represent these ideas to you.

Where ideas on one branch relate to ideas somewhere else on the Map, connect them with multi-coloured, free-flowing arrows.

If necessary, you can now add further levels with their own words, colours and pictures.

Try and use colour and images wherever possible – these stimulate your creativity and help you to think through the issues on your Map. They will also increase your information retention rate making the Map easier to recall when it is not in front of you.

Now that you have a completed (or semi-completed) Mind Map, you can go back over it and 'edit'. Try not to be too harsh on the Map (or yourself!). If some of the ideas seem obvious in retrospect, perhaps they need to be on the Map simply to reiterate what you already know.

Above all - enjoy the process. At every possible opportunity add to your Map humour, joyfulness and anything you feel that personalises it, making it inherently 'you'.

... but all of my ideas are dumb ...

There really isn't any such thing as a 'dumb' idea. There are just more and less appropriate ideas – or more and less evolved ideas. What is seemingly a 'dumb' idea may evolve into a brilliant one.

There's an old saying about writing – that in order to write a book or a story or a paper – you just have to *write*.

Your Mind Map is a brainstorming exercise. Don't worry about spelling mistakes, 'dumb' ideas, repetitive words or thoughts – write everything down, even if it seems unrelated. You never know when one seemingly mundane or unrelated idea will spark off a new idea that sets your brain on a whole different path.

Editing comes later. For now – just write.

> *... what if I get writer's block?*

Move on.

Don't get bogged down in trying to complete everything before moving on to the next bit. If you run out of ideas for one BOI, move on to the next. Perhaps draw some blank lines from the BOI to remind your brain that you're not quite done there and that it should keep thinking about information to fill in. The brain is an amazing machine – it will come up with information for whatever task you set it. Drawing a 'mental blank', as it were, is often simply the result of putting too much pressure on yourself. It's just like when you are trying desperately to remember a word that you *know* you know – it will come to you when you relax and stop thinking about it. Why? Because when you relegate the question to the subconscious mind, rather than demanding it from the conscious mind, the brain has a chance to relax and go through its memory banks.

The answer will come to you eventually. For now, just move on to the part you can do.

> *... I've been sitting here staring at the blank piece of paper for the last half hour and I just don't know how to start ...*

Walk away.

Mind Mapping is supposed to be a fun and joyous experience – not a chore. If you've become so stuck in 'getting it right' or not being sure about the whole thing that you've paralysed yourself and you're unable to move, just walk away.

Come back to it when you're feeling less stressed. Maybe even when you're a little tired and not so capable of worrying so much.

If you're still stuck, try looking at images for inspiration. Another option is to make your Mind Map a word association game. Write your topic in the centre and brainstorm all of the words you can think of that are associated with it. This should help to get your hand (and brain!) moving – often this is enough to shake you out of your self-inflicted rut.

Group Mind Mapping

The following is from an article by Exponential Growth Strategist and Managing Director of Jay Abraham Asia Pacific, Dr. Marc Dussault, entitled "*Group Mind Mapping: The most fun you'll ever have collecting information from your team.*" While this article particularly deals with Group Mind Mapping as a corporate activity, the process is sound and can easily be adapted for your own use by replacing the references to "our clients", "the market", "our competitors", "our strengths" and "our weaknesses" with topics that reflect the subject the group is studying.

To create a mind map you will need:

- Felt markers of different colours. The more distinctly different the colours, the better.
- Several large pieces of paper, minimum 1.5 x 3m. The bigger the better
- Masking tape
- A tape or CD player (that can play music loud enough that it's hard to talk)
- A dance music tape or CD, anything that is vibrant, fun, playful, and invigorating

This group exercise is best done with 6 to 10 people. The more people you have, the bigger the piece of paper you will need.

1. Place the sheet of paper on a smooth flat wall upon which you can easily write and draw.

2. Setup 5 minutes

Write down the topic of the subject you wish to Mind Map in the centre of the sheet of paper. For example it could be "our clients", "the market", "our competitors", "our strengths" or "our weaknesses". Be careful to select a word or phrase that is general and vague, yet describes the essence of what you are Mind Mapping without limiting the scope, breadth, or depth of the topic. "Our sales this month" is constraining whereas "sales" is wide ranging. Once you've done this a few times, you'll know how to focus. For now just get acquainted with the process.

3. Capture **30-45 minutes**

Explain the following "I would like you to put on paper ideas, thoughts, feelings, impressions, comments and suggestions that come to mind. You are to write one word or a very short phrase and immediately go to the next point as quickly as possible. Spread your thoughts around the page at will. Write wherever you are comfortable. Move around. Read what others are writing. Try not to duplicate what's already written. Dance, sing, bump into each other playfully. Act as though you are a 6 year old. Don't talk to each other. This is a singular exercise for now. Go!." Play the music loud. Loud enough so that people can't talk easily. Loud enough to stimulate their auditory senses. The volume will depend on who you are doing this with. In case of doubt, play it louder rather than softer.

4. Pattern interrupt **15-30 minutes**

When you see the page filling up OR people running out of ideas, stop them, tell them to turn their backs to the wall and close their eyes. Turn off the music. Tell them to take a deep breath. Replay the previous song at a lower sound level, although still loud enough to drown out any sounds from outside the room. Ask them to think about what they wrote and what they read. Let the entire song play. Nobody is to speak at this point. Ask them to continue to capture their ideas on paper until they run out of ideas, or the paper is filled up.

5. Linking **30-45 minutes**

Instruct the group as follows: "I would now like you to connect your thoughts with lines, circles, arrows, dotted lines, illustrations, bold, underlines, highlights - anything you think is appropriate. Link the thoughts and ideas together. No talking please. Connect the ideas on paper as best you can. As you do this, dance, sing and be playful. Do not add any more words or text." As they are doing this, you may want to interrupt a person who is not actively participating by bumping into them or giving them a different marker. Anything to interrupt the inactive pattern. When you feel people are running out of ideas, stop and do step number 4 again. Play loud music whenever they are Mind Mapping.

6. Consolidating 15-30 minutes

At this point, after having had a pattern interrupt, instruct the group as follows "I would now like you to consolidate the information you have written and drawn on paper. Pick a point and follow the link to as many other points/ideas as possible. Use your finger to feel your way around the poster. Get in touch with the feelings and thoughts written. Say the words, act out the words, see the words in your mind's eye. Be playful once again, dance around, play "twister" with your arms as others around you are snaking their way to other ideas. The goal is for you to capture as much of this information and consolidate it as a thought process, a collection of everyone else's thoughts. Once again, this is an individual exercise do not talk among yourselves and do not write or draw anything new". Once again, play the music loud.

7. Synthesizing 30-45 minutes

Ask people for their feedback about the exercise first.

- What did you think of this exercise?
- What did you like the most? What did you like the least?
- What did you find hard to do? Easy to do?
- What did you learn?
- What didn't you know before you started that is now obvious to you?

It is imperative that you gauge the group's response so you can learn how to make it more fun, impactful and engaging for them. The time you spend on each part of the exercise depends on the group and the time you have available. With a new group, the process should take about 3-4 hours. An experienced group can easily mind map in less than an hour.

One by one, ask each person to tell you their version of the story of what is on the piece of paper. You will not hear the same story twice. Ask them for what they draw out of the story- what it means to them, their job, their role in the project, etc. Even though the answers to the questions you wanted answered before you began should now be readily evident to you. Ask the questions anyway. Interpretations are priceless.

A group mind map like this does several things, but most importantly it engages individuals in a team activity that collects and reunites different points of view into a single document. By consolidating the information, conflicting points of view and feelings are brought to the forefront and out in the open in a non-confrontational manner. The thought process that gave birth to the conclusion is exposed and explained in non-linear ways that make sense to all of us, but that are often hard to diagnose, explain, and document.

When the exercise is successfully completed, you should have a crystal clear understanding of the key distinctions or guiding principles of the topic chosen. Your team members should all recognise everyone else's point of view and if time permits, a plan of action should emerge and be documented as well.

If you are really gung-ho, the next step would be to mind map the solution to the problem or issue you just mind mapped. To do this, take the first mind map off the wall, place it 2 or 3 metres away on the floor face-up so it can be viewed for inspiration for the second mind map. When do you stop this iterative process? When you no longer value the outcome or run out of time...

Mind Mapping with Software

The general theory behind Mind Mapping is the same, regardless of whether you do it by hand or use software. Each software package operates slightly differently and an in depth description of every software package and its uses is well beyond the intent and scope of this book.

You have seen in the example Mind Maps in this book a variety of different looks that can be easily created in one Mind Mapping application, and once you have the Mind Maps in electronic form, it is easy to re-purpose them for other forms of presentation.

Any software that you purchase should come with tutorials and user information to get you up to speed quickly on the use of that particular program. On top of this, there are many organisations that offer Mind Mapping workshops – both online and in person.

We will look at the important things to look for when choosing Mind Mapping software later in this chapter.

Hand-Drawn Mind Maps versus Mind Mapping Software

The subject of hand drawn Mind Maps versus Mind Maps created with software is a point of contention among Mind Map users.

Some Mind Mappers simply prefer to hand draw their Maps.

However, the benefits of Mind Mapping software are numerous. Primary among these is that the software saves you time by allowing you to make constant changes to your Map without having to redraw the entire thing.

A close second is the fact that Mind Mapping software can hold notes and links. A Mind Map on a piece of paper is just a single piece of paper – however, an electronic Mind Map can become a living database of links, notes and documents.

Also, Mind Mapping electronically simplifies the group Mind Mapping process – it allows group Mind Mapping to work even if the members of the group aren't in the same room!

Obviously, when discussing online and distance education, it would not be possible to effectively group Mind Map without Mind Mapping software.

Further, many Mind Mapping applications will allow you to export your Map in a number of formats – from word processing through to JPEGs. Some will even link into your presentation and project planning software, making it very easy to use your Mind Maps in a variety of different ways.

Hand Drawn	Software
Total flexibility of layout and freedom of expression	Software may limit the layout options and flexibility
Draw your own images or cut out from magazines	Images from graphic libraries, internet, scanned images etc.
Would need to recreate to use in other ways	Reuse in other formats through export functions
Difficult to share with others over a long distance	Easy to share via web and email
Need to redraw to rearrange branches	Easy to graft and move branches
What you see is what you get	Links to other documents and resources, hyperlinks to web sites, attach as much text as you like to branches
No immediately available assistance	Built in spell check, thesaurus, and even systems for suggesting new directions for your thoughts in some software
Whole map always visible	Can hide and show different branches to maintain focus
Need some artistic skill to create something nice looking	The software makes it easy to create nice looking Mind Maps

If you are not a highly talented artist (and if you don't have a lot of old art books lying around that you could tear up!) you may find it difficult to add the kind of illustrations you would like to your hand-drawn Mind Map.

Despite all of this, it is possible that if you are:

- creating a personal Mind Map (or group Mind Map where everyone is physically present);
- have plenty of time;
- artistically inclined;
- not needing to use the Mind Map as anything more than a simple Map;

hand-drawn Mind Mapping may be the way for you to go. There are certainly some very beautiful hand-drawn Maps available at various Mind Mapping communities.

Just as the choice of whether Mind Mapping is right for you is an intensely personal one, so is the choice of the medium through which you wish to construct your Mind Map.

Choosing the right Mind Mapping software package for you, requires you to ask a few questions.

How to choose the right Mind Mapping software for you

If you are interested in purchasing Mind Mapping software, the questions below will help you determine exactly what it is you are looking for – which will then help you figure out your software options.

1. How often will you / do you use Mind Mapping?

Let's be honest. If you only do a Mind Map once a year, investing in software probably isn't worth your time and effort. You can use the outline above to hand draw a Mind Map. Of course, this is a very time intensive activity. If you're going to do more than around two or three Mind Maps a year, you are best advised to purchase a software program – especially when you think about the value of your time, and the many advantages of using Mind Mapping software.

2. Your Operating System

Once you've decided that you definitely do want Mind Mapping Software, your choice will be in part defined by whether you are running an Apple Mac or a PC and then further dependant on what operating system and version you are running on that computer and the kind of memory you have available.

If you are unsure as to whether your operating system is supported by a particular software program, most software web sites have a 'system requirements' section on their downloads page, which will tell you the specifications required to run it. If you have further questions, contact the software sales team.

3. What do you need it for?

Over the course of the previous four chapters I have outlined the thoughts and findings, not only of myself but of many highly respected educational professionals on the variety of uses and the benefits of Mind Mapping.

You now need to ask yourself, realistically, what are you going to use Mind Mapping for? If you review the Mind Maps you have been working on from chapter to chapter, you'll see all of the amazing, inspirational ideas you have come up with. Now it's a matter of deciding which of these are realistic within the realms of your class, your syllabus and your life.

Will you use Mind Mapping for lesson planning? For handouts? For assignment sheets? For research? For presentations and lectures? For writing professional articles and books?

Will you share this amazing new skill with your students?

Make a list of all of the things you plan to use Mind Mapping for and look for a software program that fits this list.

4. What is your level of ICT skill?

This will also be a determining factor in the software product you first decide to choose. If your level of ICT skill is low, you may choose a relatively basic program to start out with.

As your level of confidence with Mind Mapping grows, however, it is normal for people to wish to upgrade to a more comprehensive software package – one that gives you the freedom to explore and create Mind Maps through your own inherent inquisitiveness.

The program you choose is up to you – if you worry that a complex software package is beyond your grasp, it may be better to go with a basic application. It would be a shame for you to be put off Mind Mapping and thus lose an incredible tool, due to fear that the application you are using is too advanced!

5. What price range are you looking at?

This is a determining factor, for obvious reasons. If you have no budget, it may be worth re-reading the beginning of this chapter which outlines the method for personal and group Mind Mapping by hand.

It may be possible to convince your teaching institution of the usefulness of Mind Mapping as a professional tool and as a skill for students (why not show them a copy of this book?).

Most software companies provide discounted licence fees when you purchase more than five licences of a product, and some companies also provide discounts for teachers, students and educational institutions.

6. What features do you need?

On the next page is a list of some features to be found in Mind Mapping software - read through the list and see what would be required for you as a teacher, and what would be required for your Mind Mapping software, and what features would be required as features for your students' software. There is also extra space to write other specific features you are looking for. If you are looking for particular features in software and find a program that is close to your needs, but is missing a key feature, don't be shy to ask for it - it may well already be under development, or the company may think that it's a great idea and implement it based on your request - I certainly know that we have done this in the past, and I would imagine other companies may well do the same.

Feature	Teacher	Students
Hyperlinks on branches		
Automatic / Manual branch coloring		
Checkboxes on branches		
Start/Finish date, percent complete recording/display		
Mind Map image exports		
Mind Map outline exports		
Print Mind Map without branch titles		
Outline numbering		
Background images		
Boundaries around groups of branches		
Program suggests ideas		
Localised language requirements		
Link lines between branches		
Quality graphics libraries		
Attached graphics / text		
Multiple Mind Maps in a single document		
Full screen editing		
Export to presentation software		
Built-in specialised presentation feature		
Rapid-fire data entry for brainstorming		
Built-in outline view		
Branch meaning adornments		
Task priority markers		
FlexiBranches® or similar		
Print headers and footers		
Mind Map layout assistance / free layout		

Feature	Teacher	Students

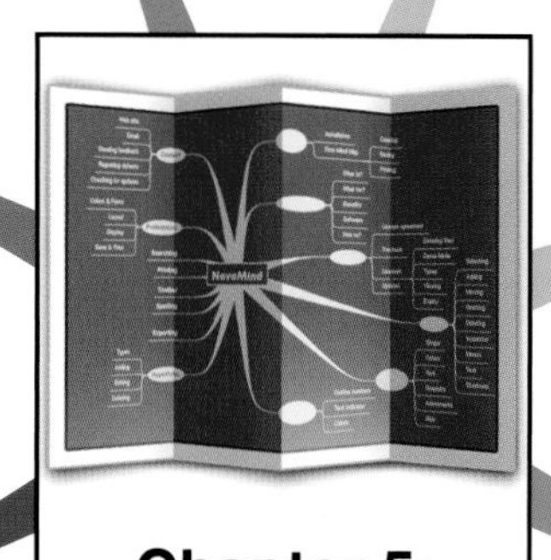

Chapter 5: Constructing Mind Maps

Chapter 6: Professional development

In Chapter 6 we will discuss:What Professional Development is; Professional Development, ICT and Mind Mapping; Mind Mapping as a Career Planning Tool; Mind Mapping as a Research Tool; Using Mind Mapping when attending seminars / workgroups; Using Mind Mapping in an Association Setting.

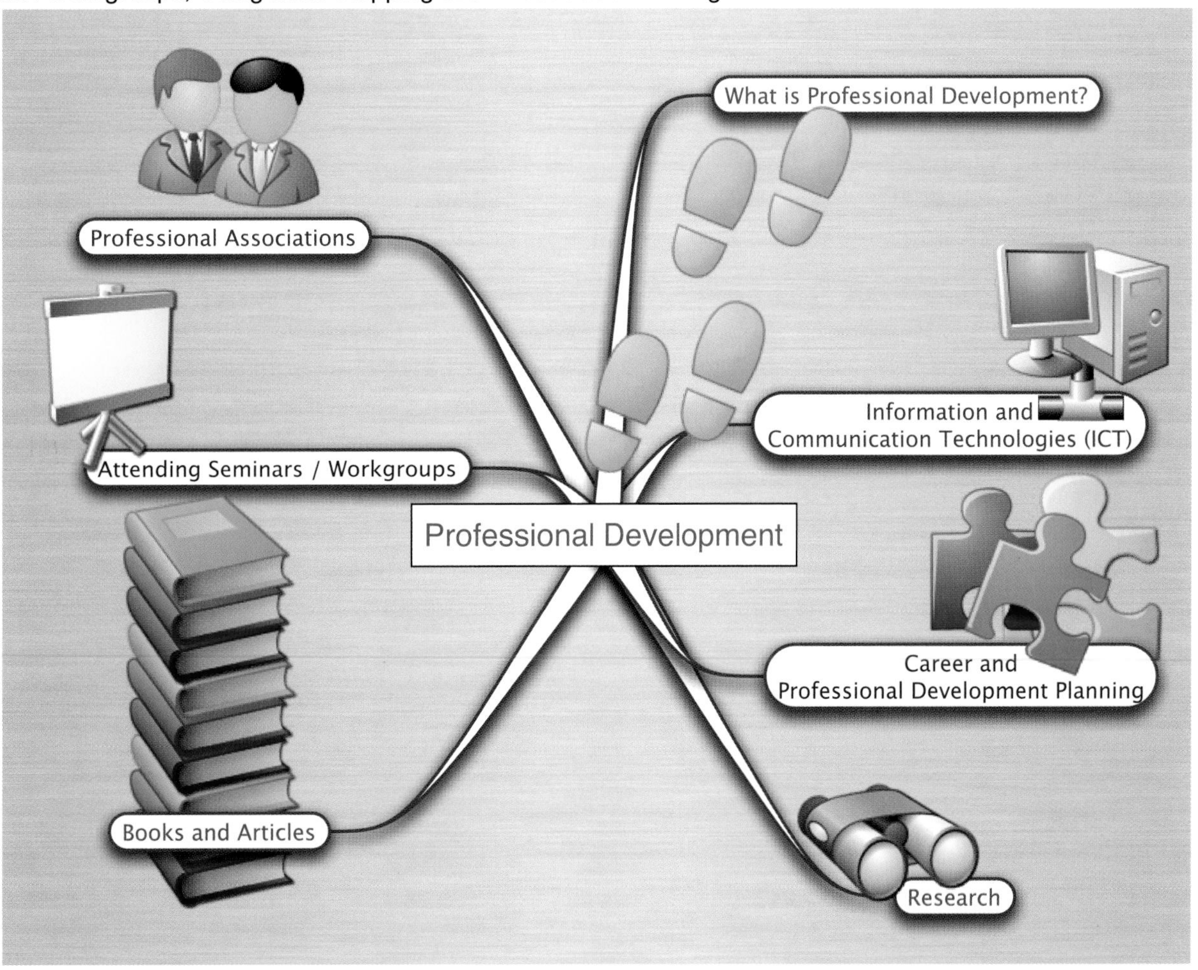

What is Professional Development?

Professional Development is the process of ongoing learning to keep up to date in ones chosen area of expertise.

Professional Development is crucial for a number of reasons. Clearly, as teachers are in the industry of knowledge, ongoing learning is an integral part of their existence. Further, Professional Development encourages new learning strategies, often via peer discussion. This peer discussion also helps some teachers to overcome feelings of isolation and fear of change.

On their web site[1], the Australian Association for the Teaching of English says that:

"Teachers need:

- *access to new research and knowledge in the teaching of literacy, language development and an integrated curriculum;*
- *appropriate, up to date qualifications in both the content area of the subject and in teaching methodology;*
- *opportunities to share expertise with other experienced teachers and educators leading to reflection on practice;*
- *opportunities for discipline renewal for teachers whose teacher education took place some years ago;*
- *a commitment at all levels to time release to attend professional development activities; and*
- *recognition at all levels of the value of professional development."*

While this refers specifically to English teachers, its sentiments are obviously applicable to educators across the board.

Further, in another statement, the Australian Association for the Teaching of English says:

"Access to professional development is crucial in enabling teachers to:

- *improve learning outcomes for students;*

1 http://www.aate.org.au/index.php?id=40

- *take a more active role in curriculum planning, including building on and refining existing practices;*
- *constantly develop excellent teaching practices;*
- *actively participate in the evaluation of teaching practices and programs; and*
- *actively participate in the implementation of local, state and national curriculum initiatives.*

For many people, the thought of having to constantly keep up to date with all the new developments is a fearful prospect, and they think that it is going to be very difficult and take over their personal time as well as taking them away from their teaching. Using Mind Mapping, the complexities of the new ideas can be easily broken down into concepts that can both be easily understood and fitted in with your existing knowledge and understanding. I recall several times when I was presented with a new computer programming concept with a whole new jargon language surrounding it, but when I had looked at it in some detail, it was "just like" something I already knew, and with the knowledge transfer that came with that association, it was easy to become thoroughly conversant with the new concepts quickly. The same is true of the new concepts for teaching in different ways – in most cases, once you Mind Map them out, you will be able to see the associations to your existing knowledge, and thoroughly "own" the information.

Attendance at professional development seminars and ongoing learning via the internet or other methods can be used in resumes in order to show a deep interest in your own profession and commitment to ongoing, continuous improvement – a key skill desired in people of all professions.

It is important, however, that you seek relevant professional development opportunities – both so that you can achieve your own personal goals and so that your record of professional development reflects your growing professional maturity and level of education. By recording the information you have learned in Mind Maps, you extend your understanding of the topics and are able to maintain an extended knowledge of a wide range of topics with minimum effort. Review of the material later is also much easier because of the visual aspects of the layout, colour, curves and images on the Mind Maps.

The Australian Association for the Teaching of English give guidelines on choosing effective learning environments and courses that will give real benefits to you – they recommend that:

"Professional development should:

- *empower participants - teachers in control;*
- *meet the identified needs of teachers, faculties and schools;*
- *be challenging;*
- *be informative;*
- *be innovative;*
- *be well planned;*
- *build skills;*
- *involve active participation;*
- *have realistic, achievable expectations;*
- *involve team work;*
- *link theory and practice;*
- *use informed presenters to share their experience or research;*
- *have a variety of approaches and styles;*
- *elicit feedback and respond to this as appropriate;*
- *be ongoing;*
- *have formative and summative evaluation processes;*

- *encourage networking; and*
- *be professionally fulfilling and enjoyable."*

In meeting these requirements, Mind Mapping is an excellent tool to identify the needs of the teachers, include interactive participation and team work, link theory and practice, encourage networking, elicit feedback, use different styles and approaches, and makes the learning fulfilling and enjoyable. So as you can see, it is an excellent tool for professional development.

Information and Communication Technologies (ICT)

It is a necessity for teachers to be up to date with current technologies – not only in their roles as educators, but also in their roles as professionals.

Those who get stuck in the past are invariably left behind.

ICT can be a particularly difficult area to stay up to date in. With the ever-increasing speed of technology, it can often seem that as soon as we master one software program it is suddenly obsolete, replaced by a new and much more complex program.

This is probably a somewhat easier concept for teachers who, by virtue of their very profession, are committed to lifelong learning. However, fear of rapid change is a common psychological barrier for most people.

A paper by the Australian Government in regards to models of teacher professional development for the integration of information and communication technology into classroom practice[2], says:

> *"There is increasing attention being given to the role of new information and communication technologies in continuing professional development. Areas of use attracting attention include: the use of multimedia to*

2 *Downes, T, Fluck, A, Gibbons, P, Leonard, R, (2001), "Making Better Connections: models of teacher professional development for the integration of information and communication technology into classroom practice", http://www.dest.gov.au/sectors/school_education/publications_resources/profiles/making_better_connections.htm*

> *provide structured learning experiences around video-based case studies of learning environments, the use of productivity tools to support teachers planning and engaging in their own or collective projects, the use of telecommunications to provide channels of communication for networking and mentoring, facilitation and support, and the use of online professional development courses and online curriculum projects that have PD embedded within them..."*

This paper states the benefits of using ICT for professional development purposes. The nature of Mind Mapping software is such that it complements a range of other ICT professional development mediums – such as online learning, both collaboratively and personally.

Further, Mind Mapping software could be considered in and of itself an ICT professional development medium, as illustrated by the statement, "the use of productivity tools to support teachers planning and engaging in their own or collective projects".

As outlined in previous chapters, Mind Mapping is very good for online learning – both in a group and individually.

The Queensland Department of Education document 'Smart Classrooms Professional Development Framework', looks at three different levels of ICT knowledge by teachers. They call these 'ICT Certificate', 'ICT Pedagogical Licence' and 'ICT Pedagogical Licence Advanced'. They define them as follows:

> ***"ICT Certificate** provides a base level for teacher ICT use. This includes some core skills, knowledge and abilities as well as ICT in a pedagogical context.*
>
> ***ICT Pedagogical Licence** acknowledges teachers who effectively integrate ICT into teaching and learning.*
>
> ***ICT Pedagogical Licence Advanced** acknowledges teachers who make ICT integral to teaching and learning and demonstrate leadership within the school. "*

If used in all of the ways outlined so far – that is, for pre-classroom, in-class and professional development projects – the process of Mind Mapping would certainly add towards a teacher being recognised as having 'ICT Pedagogical Licence Advanced'.

One of the biggest problems with moving away from the base 'ICT Certificate' is finding ICT programs that can be easily and readily adapted to a classroom setting and, further, finding interesting and creative ways to do this that fit within the curriculum and your lesson plans.

As demonstrated in Chapter 4, there are many ways in which Mind Mapping can be included in classroom activities – on an individual level, in small groups or for the class as a whole.

In fact, Mind Mapping is probably one of the easiest ICT programs to use within the classroom setting. This is because it will adapt and fit in with your current lesson plans, rather than requiring you to write new plans from scratch.

All that is required is a single lesson on how to Mind Map, although even this could be incorporated into existing lessons – Mind Mapping is a practical skill that is best learned through *doing* rather than through theory.

Pre-Service Teachers

The paper "Mathematics Learning Forum: Role of ICT in the construction of pre-service teachers' content knowledge schema"[3], explores concepts of different learning styles for student teachers, particularly as they learn to teach mathematics.

> *"Modelling involves the establishment of links among representations of a mathematical concept and its relationship to other concepts. More importantly, a model needs to externalise the links to the learner in ways that would help him or her visualise them."*

Modelling is important in any aspect of learning, in order to help the student make links between what they already know and new information and further, to present the ways in which both standing and recently acquired knowledge link.

As the above quote says, it is important that the model externalise the links in order to help the learner visualise them.

Mind Mapping is ideal for this kind of knowledge modelling.

> *"Having constructed a model for a concept, teachers could go further and consider exploration of that*

3 *Chinnappan, M (2003), "Mathematics learning forum: Role of ICT in the construction of pre-service teachers' content knowledge schema", Australian Journal of Educational Technology, 19(2), 176-191. AJET 19*

model. Model exploration could involve activities that help children gain insight into the many interwoven connections that may have been established among the relevant knowledge components of the model. Such an exploration could reveal the structure of schemas to the learner. In this way children can be expected to access higher levels of prior knowledge and attempt to integrate that knowledge with elements of the model that is being constructed. The modelling process could also contribute to the expansion of networks of schemas that are associated with mathematical concepts resulting in deeper understandings."

This is yet another, practical example of Mind Mapping in action. Using the concept of Radiant Thinking, the exploration of the model involves the extension of ideas through sub-branches, representing the semantics of the relationships and the logical linkages back to the initial knowledge components. This visual structural exploration of the model massively increases the coherence of the wider model within the student's world view.

Career and Professional Development Planning

As discussed in Chapter 4, Mind Mapping can be used as a very effective tool for career planning. This is just as applicable to teachers as it is to their students.

Career Mind Maps can be used to set goals for the future, to determine knowledge gaps and how to fill them, to reverse engineer a career path and to keep on track towards your goals.

A professional development Mind Map is a complimentary map to your career Mind Map (or, it may even be a branch from your career Mind Map). Once you have used your career Mind Map to determine your career goals, research various professional development courses, seminars and other activities. Add these to your professional development Mind Map.

Printing out these Mind Maps (in full colour, of course!) and hanging them on a wall in your study or bedroom will help you remember and stay focused on your goals.

A practical exercise for career Mind Mapping has been included in Chapter 7.

Research

It is normal for research – whether it is for lesson plans, or for writing books or articles – to be a long and complicated process. It is important to always keep track of references of quotes and information you have gathered. This can be an onerous task – particularly when you are organising research for a larger book or article.

As an advanced organiser, Mind Mapping is an ideal tool to keep track of the information you have gathered.

There are two main ways in which most teachers use Mind Maps to organise their research:

1. Information can be recorded within the Mind Map: many Mind Mapping software tools have a 'text note' function that allows you to paste information into the Map that will not be seen when the Mind Map image is printed out, but is easily available from the electronic version, and can be printed in an outline printout.

2. The Mind Map can be used as a reference database, with reference information recorded on branches. In an electronic version, this reference information can even be hyperlinked to the documents on your hard drive or the web pages that it came from, so that when you need to access the material, one click will open the hyperlinked document or page. This is the preferable option if you are dealing with large amounts of information.

Further, Mind Maps make it easy to identify gaps in information. The one page, intuitive layout allows you to see very quickly and easily anything that may be missing.

Books and Articles

Many academics publish books, articles and study papers as part of their Professional Development.

Mind Mapping can help throughout the process of writing – from planning the piece, to researching and even as a tool to help in the publishing process.

The first draft Mind Mapped book plan for this book looked like this:

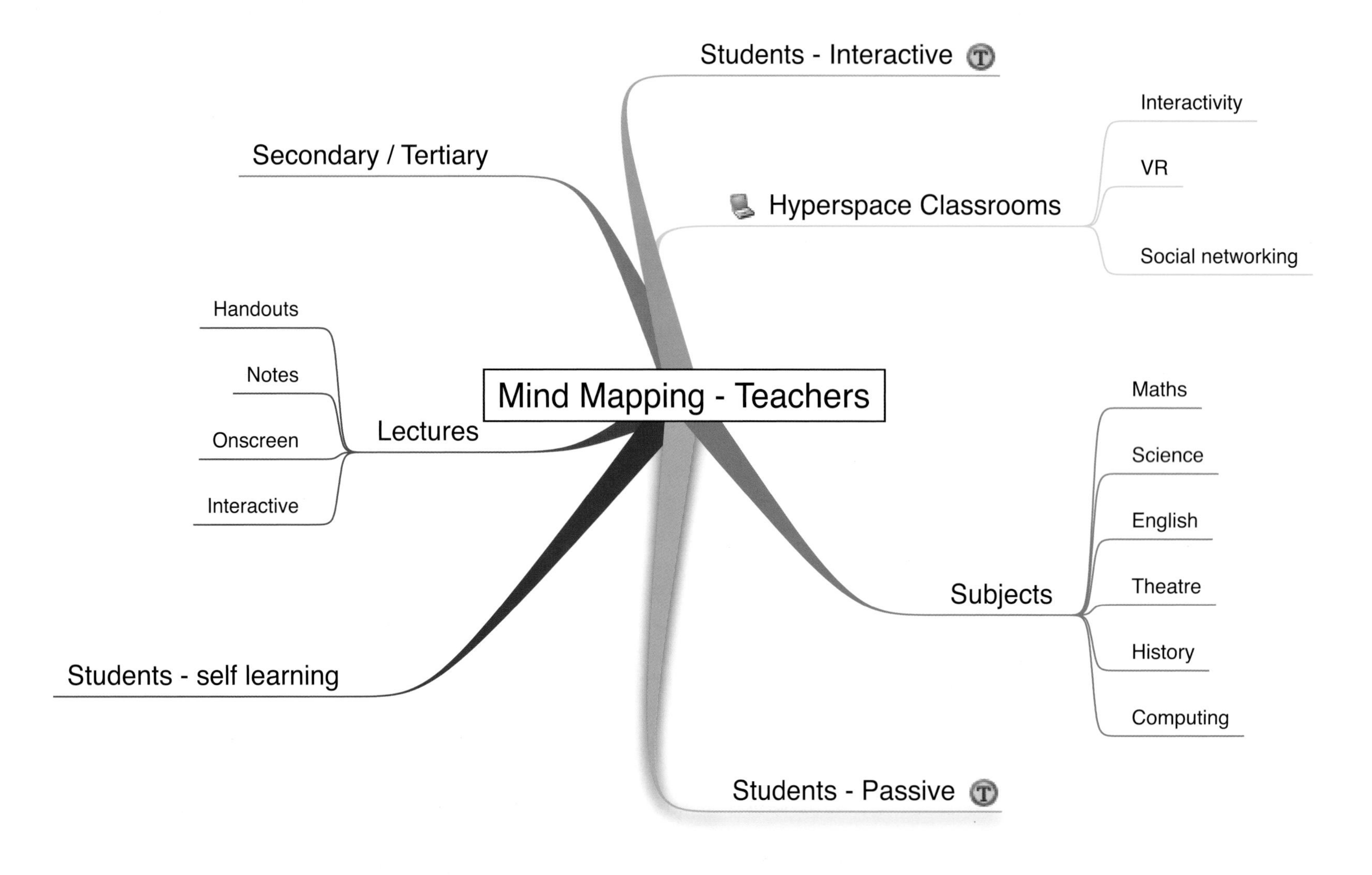

The layout of the book changed throughout the writing process, however this was a very good start to be able to figure out what information I already had, what needed to be researched and the professionals required to fill in knowledge gaps. The map evolved to represent more closely the chapter structure and detail added as the research continued.

Once the overall map had been completed, a Mind Map was created for each chapter that acted in much the same way as the overall layout Mind Map. For a project of this magnitude, it was necessary to create a separate Mind Map for each chapter – for smaller projects (papers and articles, for example) this step would probably be unnecessary.

Each of these Chapter Mind Maps was hyperlinked into the overall Mind Map.

Then, the word processing document containing the chapter text was hyperlinked into the Chapter Mind Map.

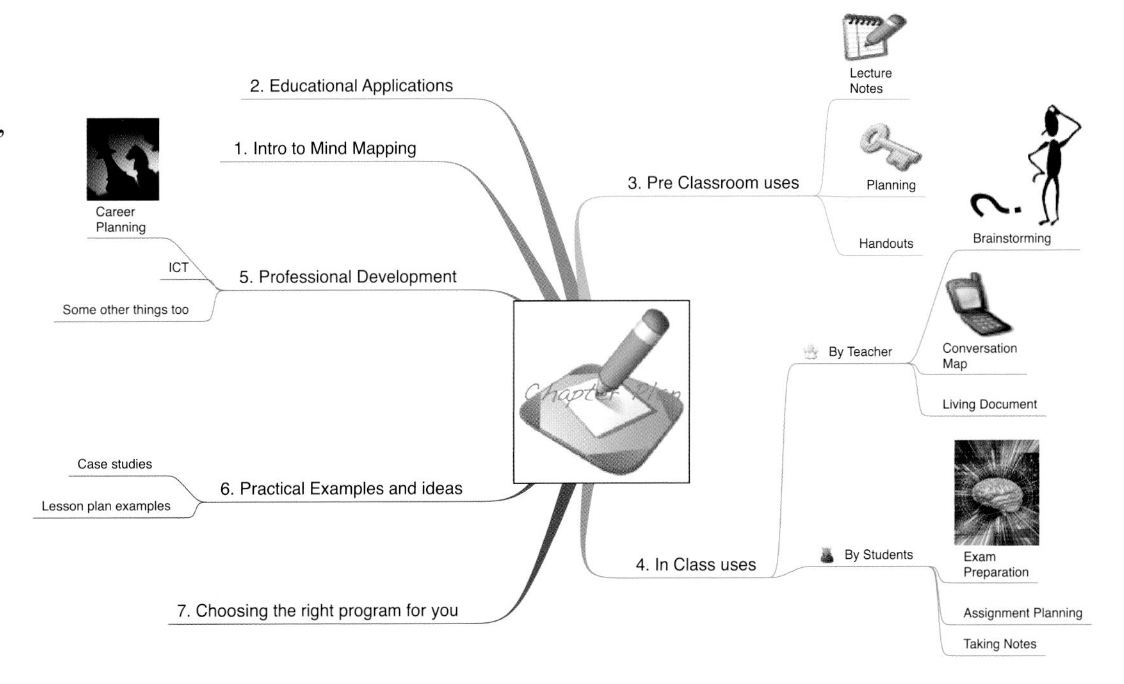

As detailed above, another Mind Map was created as a reference database, allowing easy retrieval of reference documents when they were needed throughout the writing process.

Writing the book / article / paper is then as easy as:

- Opening the overall layout Mind Map, determining which Chapter to write, clicking on the hyperlink for that chapter;
- Software automatically opens the corresponding Chapter Mind Map, clicking on the hyperlink to the word processing document;

- Opening the research database Mind Map;
- Writing in to the word processing document the information you already know;
- Filling in the gaps using the research from the research database.

As you can see, the uses of Mind Mapping software can extend well beyond making pretty, useful plans and to do lists! As a software application, Mind Mapping can be incredibly powerful and used as an organiser, a database and a presentation tool.

At the end of the process, the overall Mind Map was tidied up and used as a book overview in Chapter 1, and the individual chapter Mind Maps appear at the start of each chapter. This gives a quick visual overview of the material for both an introduction to the material and a quick reminder review and index to information when used as a reference later.

An updated version of a Mind Map like the one in the start of this book would be an excellent inclusion in a proposal to publishers as it summarises your entire book on one page – allowing publishers to decide quickly and readily if the content is of interest to them.

Writing papers and articles, while perhaps not quite as in depth a process as writing a book, can also benefit from Mind Mapping through the planning, writing and publishing stages.

In fact, when you have completed your article, you could even use a Mind Map to record the submission process. Begin by using the BOI's to list all publications (hard copy or online) that may be interested in your article. This is a crucial step. Submitting an article that is not relevant to a publication may earn you the ire of the editor – which could be particularly troublesome if you had another, more relevant article to submit to them at a later date.

Once you have listed the publications, solicit submission information from each of them (some publications will have this information on their web site. Always check this before contacting them directly) and record this on your Mind Map.

When you submit your article to the publications, be sure to update your Mind Map with the date the article was sent and who it was addressed to. This will make follow-up easier.

Attending Seminars / Workgroups

Attending conferences, seminars and workgroups can be an excellent way to learn about new teaching strategies and to network with peers.

If you are like most attendees, however, you may find that you often leave these events with pages and pages of notes that you never get a chance to organise and thus use effectively.

This is because notes, especially handwritten notes, taken in a linear, hierarchical format are not intuitive and do not appeal to you on a basic level.

By Mind Mapping your notes during the seminar, you will find them easier to read and you will find the information disseminated through the seminar much easier to recall. Also, the information is often presented out of logical order, or one presenter may provide information that links to information that has already been presented. Linear note-taking totally misses the links and associations, but with Mind Mapping, you can easily extend the existing branches with sub-branches for the new information, recording it in a logically coherent form for more effective use later.

Liner note-taking totally misses the links and associations, but with Mind Mapping, you can easily extend the existing branches with sub-branches for the new information, recording it in a logically coherent form for more effective use later.

If you are not comfortable with Mind Mapping during the seminar, or if you are unable to do so, you could also you a Mind Map to organise your notes afterwards.

There are two options on this front. You can either Mind Map from memory and then go back over your notes and add in any relevant information that you have left out, or you can Mind Map using the notes you have taken as a guide.

This is best done immediately after the seminar, while the information is still fresh in your mind.

It is worthwhile encouraging your peers and colleagues to Mind Map. If you attend a seminar with another person and both Mind Map your notes and share them afterwards, the results are twice as good! If you attend with several other people and you *all* Mind Map and compare Maps afterwards, the results can be amazing!

Group Mind Mapping within seminars is also a useful exercise, regardless of whether you are the seminar teacher or student. The process for Group Mind Mapping is outlined in Chapter 5.

Professional Associations

Membership in professional associations is an excellent way of keeping up to date with advances in and information on your industry.

Mind Maps have several uses within an association setting. As outlined in 'Seminars and Workgroups' earlier, Mind Mapping works well for taking notes and for group brainstorming exercises. However, they also make very good meeting agendas.

You can even take minutes using Mind Maps, in much the same way that you would use Mind Mapping to take notes. You start with the meeting agenda Mind Map and as the meeting progresses, you branch out to the actual topics, decisions, and assignments that were decided during the meeting. You then immediately have clear and concise notes available for instant distribution.

Once distributed, you will see that these minutes are unlike ordinary minutes, which often are distributed, opened once, never read and never looked at again. Using Mind Maps for the meeting minutes, all the information is available at a glance, and people can see where their part of the responsibilities fits in to the overall scheme of things.

A Mind Map will interest association members and will save them precious time by quickly, easily and intuitively outlining everything they need to know.

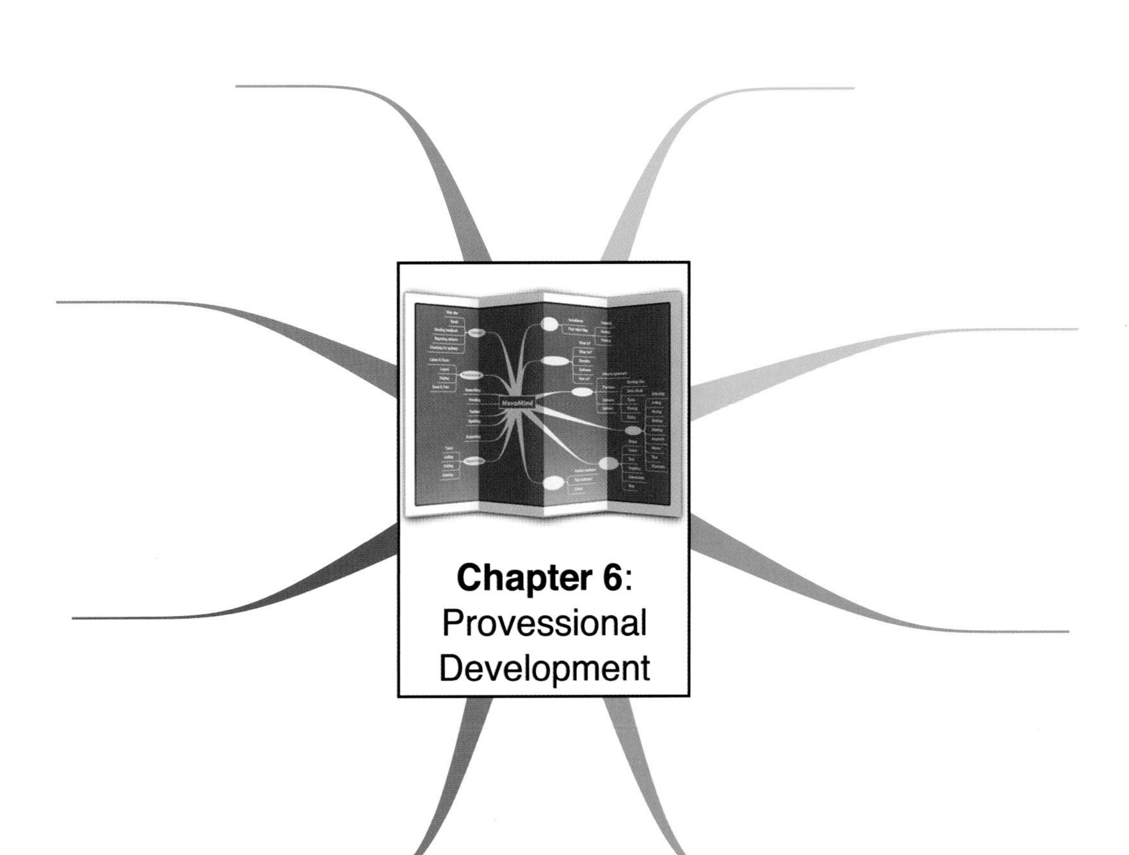
Chapter 6:
Provessional
Development

Chapter 7: Practical Examples and Ideas for the Classroom

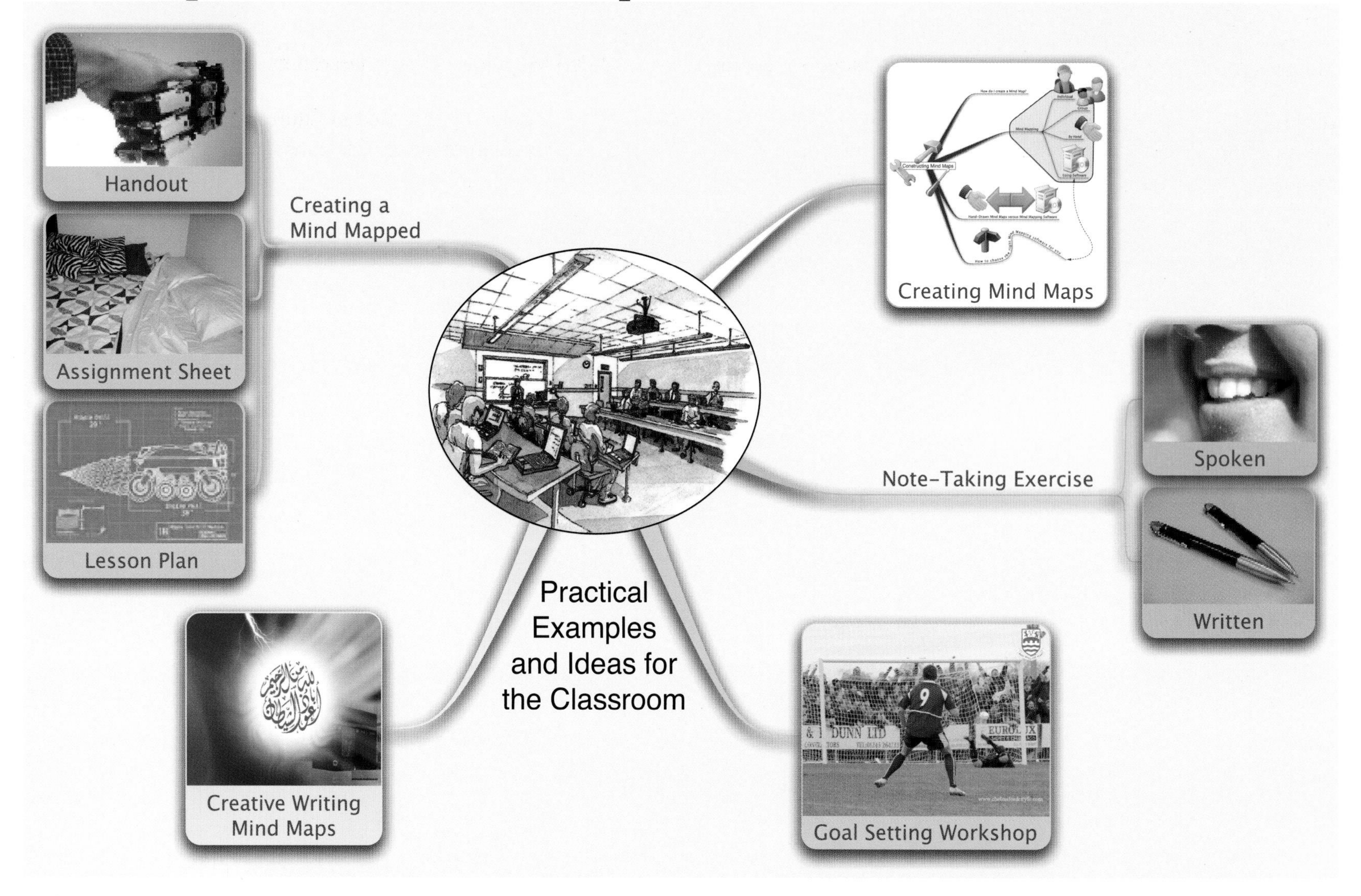

This chapter has been provided as a practical background to give you ideas on how to specifically incorporate Mind Mapping – both into your classroom and into your life.

Many of these lesson plans were provided by teachers who currently use Mind Mapping in their classrooms.

If you find any of these lesson plans particularly useful, or if you have plans that could be included in future editions of this book, please contact the author with this information as I am looking at constant improvement to make this chapter an even more valuable resource for teachers everywhere.

Creating Mind maps

Provided by: **Young People's Commission for Africa**

Target: Students

Objective: For students to create a mind map of their impressions of the continent of Africa

The students will:

- Participate in a class discussion of their impressions of Africa
- Work in groups to continue the discussion
- Work together as a class to create a mind map
- Decide how they wish to display their ideas

Cross Curricular Links

KS3 Citizenship

Starter Activity

Explain what a mind map is.

Development

Break into groups of 5 or 6 and discuss what they think are the defining features of the continent.

Each group presents their ideas to the class.

Plenary / Extension Work

Lead the class as they create a giant Mind Map around the word 'Africa.'

How to display your work

There are several different ways:

- Create your work in a Mind Mapping program.
- Do the work by hand and then scan
- Use an interactive whiteboard

Extension - Making more of the mind map

The class may illustrate the ideas on their mind map by placing photographs, illustrations, and links to relevant web sites.

For example, they can:

- Take photographs to illustrate their ideas using the digital camera and upload them.
- Scan photographs and pictures out of books and magazines.
- Copy quotes from literature, magazines or newspapers which are good representations of their views.
- Write up quotes from the class discussion.
- Write their own one-line statements.
- Write short opinion pieces.
- Write short poems.

Note Taking Exercise - Spoken

Target: Students

Objective: Teaching your students to take lecture notes with Mind Maps

Begin by letting the students know the title or central theme of the piece they are taking notes on and also the main topics within the talk – this simplifies the process, allowing them to concentrate on the note taking process rather than trying to guess what the central theme and topics will be!

Have the students place the central theme in the centre of the circle and draw branches for each of the main ideas.

If this is the first time you have introduced Mind Mapping to your students, it may even be worth providing a printed handout with spaces for the central theme and the branches already on it to help them see how a Mind Map should be laid out. They can then fill in the spaces themselves. Some Mind Mapping programs allow you to make a Mind Map and print it out without the text for exactly this purpose.

As you speak, have students record their impressions, distinctions and thoughts on the Map. Remind them that this is not a regular note taking exercise – they are not to write down every word that you say, nor even summarise it. Instead, they should choose key words or pictures to represent *their understanding* of what is being said.

Once they have finished with this exercise, students should spend some time going over their Maps, with your guidance. They should have time to clarify with you any points they may have missed or information that they are unsure how to interpret.

Have students hand in their Maps and return them at a later date (perhaps a week later). Students should spend some time looking at their Map and seeing how much of the information they can recall without prompting.

This exercise will show that not all students find Mind Mapping as the most beneficial method of note taking. There are students for whom traditional note taking is ideal. However, studies show that a high percentage of students will benefit from taking notes in this method. Also, since it is a change from what most students are used to, often they need to use the Mind Mapping techniques several times to see whether they work well for them.

Some ideas for students to practice outside of class so that they become more comfortable with the process of taking notes with Mind Mapping:

- Mind Map the television news while watching it;
- Create Mind Maps from notes that students have taken previously (advice on this follows in the next exercise);
- Students could work with someone else, so that while one person is Mind Mapping the lecture, the other person is taking normal notes – these can then be compared after class.
- If students are still uncomfortable with their ability to get all of the relevant information down during the lecture, they may wish to record it so that they can replay and fill in anything they have missed at a later date.

Note Taking Exercise - Written

Target: Students

Objective: Teaching your students turn their written notes into a Mind Map

Students can either use notes they have taken previously for this exercise, or instead they may wish to use it to summarise a book, article or report.

Begin by having students read over the piece they are going to Mind Map.

Next, they should place the central theme at the centre of the Map. Having read the piece, they should be aware of the central theme. However, if they have trouble distinguishing it they may want to use the title or read the blurb or abstract. Where students are Mind Mapping their own notes, the title of the lecture is probably a good place to start. The picture for the central theme may be suggested by the cover or graphics or images within the material.

Students can determine the Basic Ordering Ideas by looking at chapter headings, subtitles or division headings or, in the case of their own notes, by highlighting these ideas as they read through their notes. A good indicator to look out for when searching for your Basic Ordering Ideas is the heavy incidence of a particular word in a small section of the notes.

From here, students should fill in what they feel is the most important and relevant information, ensuring that they don't just place information in because it seems to fit – the Map must be practical and must therefore be personal, it should appeal to the student and should hold what they feel is important and relevant, not just what they are told is.

This will help your students to build experience in summarising important information and confidence in identifying what that information is.

Encourage them to use lots of colour and graphics in their Map to help them improve their retention and recall rate.

As in the earlier note taking exercise, the first time you work on this with students it may be useful to collect the Maps at the end and hand them out some time later. This allows students to see how much of the information they can recall and therefore how effective either Mind Mapping is for them or how useful their particular Map actually is.

Goal Setting Workshop

Target: Teachers - Professional Development

Objective: To establish a five year career plan

Place your particular goal in the centre of the Mind Map. Your goal may be physical: a particular posting, job title; material: salary range, buying a house, a car, going on holidays; or it may be more esoteric: wanting to contribute to the community, teaching in a third world country, working with disabled children.

Now, for ten minutes, without correcting or critically analysing what you are writing, create lines (or 'branches') from the central idea and brainstorm anything that comes to mind that would lead to that goal – education, networks, people – it can be obvious, impossible, outrageous … this is brainstorming, only you will be reading it – go crazy! Write for the full ten minutes without stopping.

Once your ten minutes are up, walk away from your Map for a little while – whether this is ten minutes, an hour or a day. Come back to it and begin thinking about what you've written.

At this point, it is certainly much easier to go through this process if you have Mind Mapping software as this allows you to make changes, move things, delete things, and add things without having to redraw the entire map. It also makes it very easy to add colour and pictures.

Group the things you think are 'impossible' or 'useless' to one side – don't delete them! You never know when they will become 'useful' and 'possible'.

Narrow your Map and work on it until you are happy that you have a clear path mapped out. To do this, you may need to conduct research or talk to colleagues. Ensure that you record all of the results of this research in your Map.

Make sure that you use plenty of colours and key words – cut out pictures from magazines that represent your goals if you are Mapping by hand or copy and paste pictures from the internet if you are using software.

When you feel happy with what you have produced, print it out (if you are using software) and hang it on the wall in a prominent position. This step is important – you want to stay focused on your goals by having them around you. You may even want to make a smaller version of your Map that you can carry with you.

This kind of Mind Map needs to be revised on a regular basis. For the first week, read it through every day, making any changes that feel right to you, then read it once a week for the next month, and then once a month after that. At the end of 6 months, create a new Mind Map, looking at your existing one only for the title. Critically assess whether the goal is still relevant and suitably stated. Now create your new Mind Map without referring to the old one, and using the same brainstorming techniques. Once you have finished, compare your two Mind Maps and see what the similarities and differences are. Note how the priorities have changed. This will help you to constantly refine your direction so that it matches your current position, and any new information you have learned. Remember to reward yourself for your accomplishments as you achieve them and mark them on your Mind Map so you remember them every time you review the Mind Map. Continue the review procedure and full rewrites every 6 months to keep everything relevant and focused. Have fun – make it a joyous process. You are, after all, designing your life – it should be an enjoyable, creative and stimulating exercise!

Creative Writing Mind Maps

Provided by: Leela Cosgrove

Target: Students – 8-12 year olds

Objective: Students studying creative writing use these Mind Maps to plan their long short stories (over 2,000 words)

Students begin by determining what their story is going to be about and who the main character will be. They write a short, linear plan of the beginning, middle and end of the story (these only need to be a sentence each).

Students Mind Map everything that is going to happen in their story. This doesn't have to be in any kind of linear format – encourage them to just write down everything they think of that could happen to their character between the beginning of the story and the end of the story, telling them that they can sort it out later.

Once the ideas have been Mind Mapped, students move the ideas around, delete those which aren't necessary and that don't fit and add anything extra that needs to happen.

At this point, I normally have students print out their Mind Map and stick it in the front of their writing journal. As my classes are weekly and the story will be written over a number of months, the Mind Map will grow and evolve as their story does. Printing out a new copy of it each time it changes is a really good way for students to later track the evolution of their story and to use it as a base to analyse the writing process.

Creating a Mind Mapped Lesson Plan

Target: Teachers – Planning

Objective: The below are three different ways in which three different teachers Mind Map their lesson plans.

Provided by: Hazel Wagner

1. Define Subject.
2. Brainstorm ideas around the main subject.
3. Print off Mind Map for handing out to students – I like to leave plenty of white space so students can write their notes right on the mind-map. It gets them practice with mind-mapping and proves the value of taking notes in that form.

Provided by: Craig Turner

1. Define Subject--Movement Training for Actors.
2. Research Subject--Acting Process; Mind body research; Trance-state performance; Mask; Stage Combat (all these and others, taking notes and incorporating into a sequence of training).
3. Collate Research and open Mind Mapping Program--I use DevonThink Pro to collect and categorize themes/ideas/topics and then export to NovaMind.
4. Brainstorm ideas around the main subject--This is something I do a lot of in NovaMind. It lets me shift ideas and topics around, to see their relationship(s), and to make a coherent whole approach to a lesson/training sequence.

5. Analyse the subject – its size and relevancy.

6. Using research, fill in any information gaps, Mind Mapping helps me see the gaps.

7. Print off Mind Map for handing out to students.

Provided by: Mark Gilchrist

1. Look at (commercial) scheme of work.

2. Define objectives, main steps, resources and notes.

3. Map it out to act as an aid to my failing memory!

You could also use a template such as this to plan the desired outcomes (so you know what you are aiming for), the assignments, activities and homework, and how you are going to assess whether the lesson was successful and how to improve it for next time, and how to assess whether the outcomes were achieved by the students.

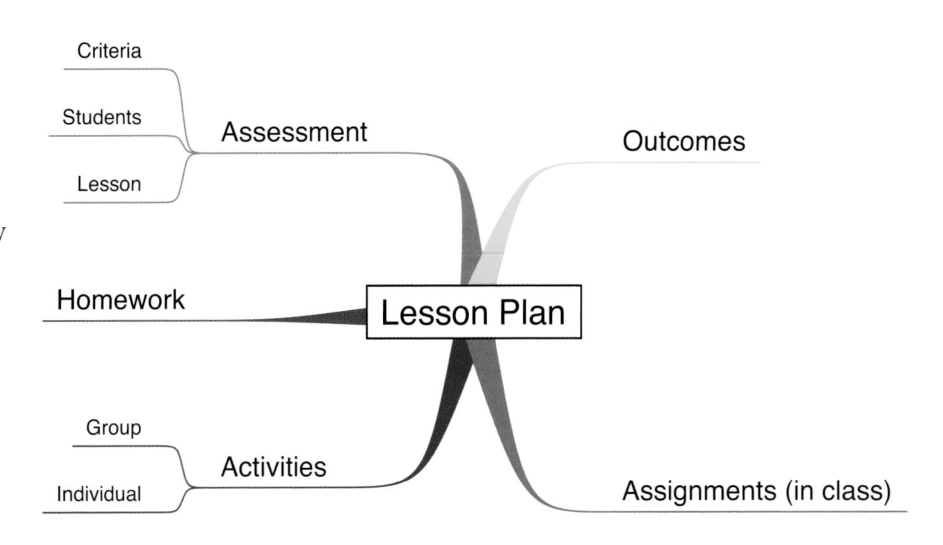

Creating a Mind Mapped Handout

Target: Teachers – Planning

Objective: To create a Mind Mapped handout for your students

Provided by: Mark Gilchrist

1. Identify the overall map.
2. Produce a starter map.
3. Project via PC and data projector.
4. Pen in other ideas.
5. Allow students to complete.

Provided by: Hazel Wagner

1. Build my mind map in the subject of the day.
2. Add all the details to the mind map that I need.
3. Make a copy of the detailed mind map for me to use as I teach.
4. Make copies of the mind map without the details and with room for students to make notes as the hand-out.

Provided by: Craig Turner

1. Easy: I simply output the Map as a JPEG image for paper distribution or inclusion in class materials.

2. (there is no step 2)

Creating a Mind Mapped Assignment Sheet

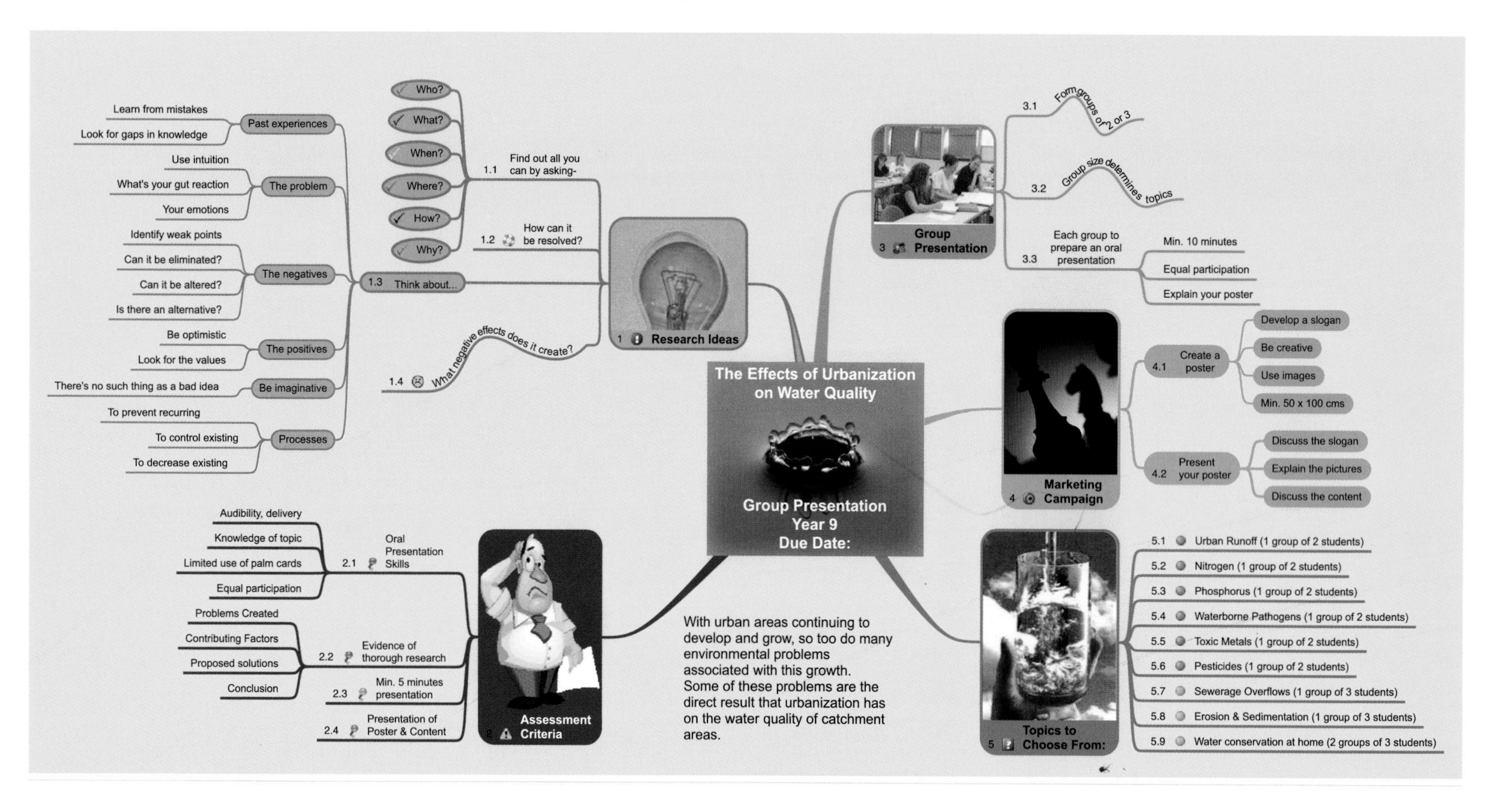

Target: Students

Objective: Replaces the traditional Assignment Sheet

The on the previous page shows an assignment sheet for a Year 9 group presentation assignment.

Using the above as a template, create your own assignment sheet by doing the following:

Put the assignment title and due date in the centre.

Use a separate branch for each part of the assignment – in the example above, there are branches for:

- The topics that may be chosen;
- The two parts of the assignment – a marketing campaign and a group presentation;
- Some research ideas;
- Assessment criteria.

It is important to list all of the assessment criteria on one branch – this allows students to easily compare their assignment against the marking criteria before they hand it in.

Be sure to use colours and graphics – this will make the Map more appealing and will improve information retention.

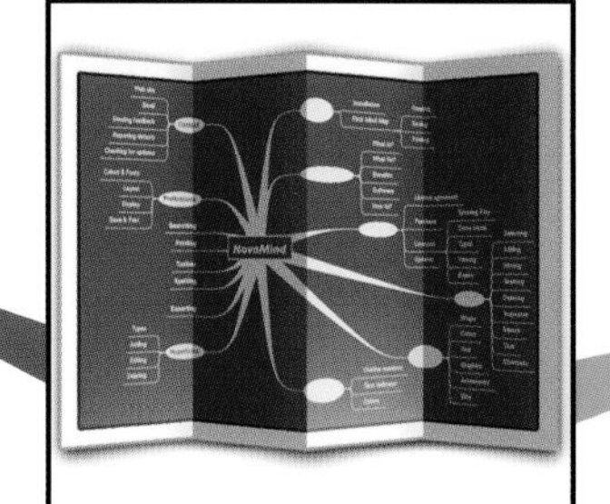

Chapter 7: Practical Examples and Ideas for the Classroom

Chapter 8: Resources

Common Mind Mapping Terms

Adornment	A small icon that is attached to the left end of a branch to visually denote some sort of special meaning.
Assisted Layout	A setting which tries to keep your Mind Map looking nice, while still allowing you to adjust the position of the branches.
Attached Graphics	Images or shapes that are attached to a branch and move when the branch is moved, but are physically separate from the bounds of the branch itself and can be moved independently of the branch, and put in front of or behind the branch.
Basic Ordering Ideas (BOI)	The main subjects, or main branches, that appear around the Mind Map's central image.
Branch	A graphical representation of an idea that is attached to either the Mind Map title, or another branch. It has either text or images (or both) to denote meaning.
Canvas	The background that the Mind Map is drawn on.
Child Branch	A branch that is below the one being discussed (further from the Title).
Collapse Symbol	A small icon that is shown at the end of the branches, which you can click to hide the children of a branch. When a branch's children are hidden, there is an Expand icon which will show the children when clicked.
Context Sensitive Menu	The menu (either traditional text style, or graphical icons) that is displayed when you right-click on your Mind Map. Different menus are displayed when editing text, clicking on a branch, or clicking on the canvas.
Controlled Layout	A setting where the program controls the placement of the branches in order to minimise the space taken by the Mind Map while making sure that the branches don't overlap.
Detail Level	The number of levels of the Mind Map that are shown - for example if the detail level is 2, the First Level Branches and their children will be shown, but any children of theirs will be hidden.
Document	A file which is displayed in a window, and contains one or more Mind Maps

First Level or Top Level branch	A branch that is attached to the Mind Map Title.
FlexiBranch®	A branch that can be reshaped using handles, while the text flows along the curve of the branch (registered trademark and patented by NovaMind).
Free Layout	A setting which does not restrict you putting your branches wherever you like on your Mind Map.
Graft	Move a branch so that it is the child of a different parent branch.
Hyperlink	A link that, when clicked, takes the user to another branch, another Mind Map, another file, or web site, or composes an email - it is a way of linking a branch to some other information either locally or remotely.
Kerning	The spacing between characters that are typed.
Link Line	A flexible line that connects branches and graphics to show other associations besides the main hierarchical organisation of the Mind Map.
Mind Map	A visual diagram representing related ideas, concepts, or tasks in a hierarchical format.
Mind Map Title or Root	The central topic of the Mind Map. There is always one of these on every Mind Map. This ensures that the Mind Map always has a single outline interpretation, unlike concept mapping.
Outline View or Outline Format	A representation of the Mind Map in text form where the branches at successive levels are indented according to their level (number of parent branches between them and the Mind Map Title).
Parent Branch	The branch above the branch under consideration in the hierarchy.
Radiant Thinking	The theory that the brain does not work in linear patterns but rather has associations from one idea radiating out through many connections.
Rainbow Colouring and Rainbow Saturation	Automatic colouring of branches depending on their location in relation to the centre of the Mind Map. This allows for quick and easy creation of colourful Mind Maps. Colours can be overridden for any branch. The Rainbow Saturation is the intensity of the rainbow colours.

Sibling Branch	A branch that is at the same level as the branch under consideration. Two branches are siblings if they have the same parent.
Snap Lines	Lines that appear as you are moving branches around which indicate when the branch you are moving is close to being aligned to another branch, or is an equal distance from the other branch. If you let the branch go while the snap line is showing, the branch will move to align with the position shown by the snap line.
Tool Palette	The small floating window that can be displayed to speed common operations like adding branches.

About the Author

The Story of NovaMind

How it all started

It was a dark, cold and lonely night when, suddenly, a flash of inspiration changed my life forever...

Actually, it was daytime and stinkin' hot. I was living in Malaysia, working as Chief Technical Officer (CTO) and Vice President of an international software company. A couple of planes had recently flown into some big buildings across the other side of the world and I was living in a Muslim country. Amongst the ex-patriot population, there was a fair amount of speculation - would there be attacks against Westerners in Malaysia? Was there a risk to our safety living there?

The company I was working for had close ties to the highest levels of US intelligence and kept us appraised of developments. We had plans to move quickly, should that be necessary - it kind of helps when your company owns a fleet of aeroplanes. Anyway, the tension was getting to my partner at the time. She felt in danger and, even though there had been no actual attacks, she wanted to move out for a few weeks with the children to let things settle down.

We decided to take them to Australia, since both her parents and mine live there, even though I was born and raised in New Zealand, until she felt it was safe to return. I had just signed up for a fifteen month contract and couldn't easily get out of it. We went to Australia and while there, my partner had a mole on her leg checked out. It turned out to be a melanoma - very serious if not removed. She underwent surgery to remove it and the procedure left a cut in her leg which was going to take some time to heal. My commitments in Malaysia meant I could not stay long to help, but the people at our church were really wonderful, helping her out as the wound was healing.

The Vision

So, there I was, back in Malaysia for the first weekend without my family. Work was hectic and seemingly a constant battle of communication and performance issues and little progress. We had dreams of staying a couple more years in Malaysia, then working in the UK for two or three years (I'm three quarters English and one quarter French) and then a couple of years in the USA before deciding where to settle down. All of that went out the window, with my partner saying that she would not live in the UK or the USA due to fear of further terrorist incidents.

Things were pretty quiet in the apartment and I didn't really have any close friends in Malaysia, so it was time to sit down and plan out the next phase of my life. Up until this point, life had just happened to me - opportunities would come up and I would take them, but I had no real plan as to what I was going to do in the short, medium, or long term, or any thoughts as to what legacy I would leave for my family or for the world.

I started jotting down ideas and pretty soon I had a mess of notes that made little sense and had no real direction. I decided to try and organise them. I got out a big sheet of paper and started drawing a Mind Map of where I was at that time and where to go from there, particularly planning what I would do for income when my contract ran out – I didn't want to renew it and have to spend more time away from my children.

I had been a contractor for some time and felt that it was time to make the big move to being my own boss. I brainstormed some ideas and part way through the process, a blinding flash of vision came to me - why not create a Mind Mapping program so that other people could easily solve their problems and come up with their own empowering plans?

Development Plans

At the time, Mac OSX had just been released and as I had done a lot of development work using NextStep and WebObjects, I was very familiar with the technology and absolutely loved it. It was so far ahead of the things I had to use at work, it was ridiculous – there I was, having to use archaic tools to develop web applications when they could have been developed in 1/10 of the time using Apple's tools.

I looked at the Mind Mapping software market on Macs and found that there were few offerings. What was offered was of low quality and feature set was pathetic. Most of all, the maps produced looked **ugly!**.

People need powerful and beautiful Mind Maps so that you can get the full benefit and impact of them and I wanted to provide this for as many people as I could. I started developing NovaMind in my weekends and evenings and released the first commercial version in August 2002. One of my biggest buzzes at the time was when a customer bought the program while it was still in beta testing!

In December 2002 I finished my full time contract in Malaysia and moved to Australia to be with my family. I kept a part time contract with the company in Malaysia to guarantee some sort of income while NovaMind was developed to the stage where it could provide an income and to provide seed money to build a company around it.

2003 saw the continued growth of the company and recruitment of staff, particularly in the business development, testing, support and office administration areas, to support the development team and get the news about NovaMind out to the world (along with the translation into Dutch, French, German, Italian, Spanish and Swedish).

2004 saw the implementation of a number of new features including Screen Writers (for movie, TV and play scripts etc.), Flexi-Branches™, Branch Proposal System™, export to HTML, Mind Manager Import/Export, export to PowerPoint, addition of hundreds of new adornments, implementation of the graphics library, translation into Japanese and Chinese and so much more.

Early in 2005 we looked at the state of the application and although the version of NovaMind we had on the market at that time was far better than anything else, we are passionate about providing absolutely the best possible for our customers. In order to do that, it was necessary to rewrite all the internals of NovaMind from the ground up - a massive undertaking, but one that has allowed us to add many new features we would not have been able to do with the old structure. It also allowed us to pave the way for the Windows version of NovaMind.

2006 saw some exciting innovations within NovaMind, including the final touches being put into NovaMind 3 and the roll out of the Windows version. We have added many new features, like the spotlight searching, branch boundaries, new line styles and we will be continuing to add many more features as we go forward.

2007 has continued to see massive changes to NovaMind, where we completely rewrote the internals of NovaMind for Windows, and proceeded to develop the Express, Pro, and Platinum editions to make the type of functionality our vastly diverse customers need available.

The Team

I would like to extend my thanks to the many people who have helped NovaMind – either as full time staff, contractors, or in various other capacities: (in no particular order) David, Matt, Florian, Lloyd, Patrick, Andrew, Ben, Ernesto, Katherine, Olivia, Rebecca, Damian, Jay, Chantelle, Anthony, Michele, Ralph, Margaret and Tony, and a special thank you to Leela for all the work she has put into this book. And most importantly to our customers, beta testers, translators and to the many people who have taken the time and made the effort to give us feedback to enable us to continue to grow and improve NovaMind.

My Personal Journey

My focus continues to grow and expand and I ask myself every day "How can I continue to develop, share and teach my success methods and tools to even more people in a fun and loving way?" The answers to this question have led me on a voyage of self discovery, sharing and building communities of people who also want to improve their lives. It has enabled me to overcome all the obstacles in my life and design the amazing life I am now living. The outworking of these philosophies are reflected in the continued development of NovaMind, my involvement with various communities online and offline and the series of books with the working title of "Design Yourself; Invent Your Future", which I am working on at the moment. You can find out more about it at http://www.invent-your-future.com/

I have gone from having a single income as a contractor to:

- Having an interest in multiple businesses, including NovaMind software – which I am happy to share the income from through our affiliate program - see http://www.nova-mind.com/Reseller for details.

- Being in the only multi-level marketing system that I have examined where I believe in the product and the remuneration is excellent – I strongly recommend this both for its health benefits and for a great source of passive income – see http://www.mymonavie.com/gideon for more information about how you can benefit from this too.

- Investing in properties.

- Share and option trading.

- Writing books such as this one and the Design Yourself; Invent Your Future series - see http://www.invent-your-future.com/ for more information.

Of course, that is only one part of life, and in that time I have also:

- Lost 25kg (55lb) of weight, and significantly improved my physical fitness.

- Faced up to the things that were not working in my life, where I was living other people's values instead of my own, and totally changed my direction in life, including getting out of a 14 year marriage that was not right from the start.

- Travelled the world, including in the last year, a cruise around Asia with 9 millionaires, shopping in Singapore, elephant riding in Thailand, going to Hong Kong just for dinner with a friend at The Peak and soaking in hot pools in New Zealand. I have now travelled to over 40 countries.

- Met Bill Clinton, Sir Richard Branson, Donald Trump, and many other very successful people. Had lunch with Randall Pinkett ("Apprentice" winner) in New York and dinner with Bill Rancic (another Apprentice winner) at a vineyard in New Zealand. Attended the World Business Forum in New York.

- Went to the Formula 1 Grand Prix as a guest of Ferrari, hosted in their corporate lounge right above pit lane, and went to the formula 1 ball and other exclusive Ferrari events.

... and many many other things I could mention – but if you want to know how you can achieve the same level of success and happiness, it's all in the books. One thing I am passionate about is sharing whatever information and tools I can with as many people as I can, and plan to accomplish that through my books, NovaMind, and whatever other media and tools are effective.

I wish you great success with Mind Mapping, whether you use it for designing your ideal life, solving problems, coming up with creative ideas, writing your screenplay, planning a project, preparing a presentation, taking your teaching skills to the next level, empowering your students, or any other use.

Mind Mapping Online Resources

Mind Mapping Communities

Some specific software applications have their own user support forums. If you are already using a software program, try checking its web site for a user forum. Otherwise, following is a list of forums and blogs that discuss Mind Mapping and that are great places to obtain and share information on the subject.

Description:	**Web Address:**
Software Company Nova Mind's Online Community:	http://www.nova-mind.com/Forum/
Chuck Frey's informative Mind Mapping Blog is packed full of information:	http://mindmapping.typepad.com/
An excellent source of information on all things IT:	http://blogs.ittoolbox.com/

Mind Mapping and Education Information

The following web sites were instrumental in the research, writing and compilation of this book. They provide excellent information and practical examples of Mind Mapping and will be of use to anyone wishing to learn more about the subject:

Description:	Web Address:
Innovation Tools	http://www.innovationtools.com/index.asp
Mind Tools	http://www.mindtools.com/
University of Minnesota, Digital Media Center	http://dmc.umn.edu/activities/mindmap/
James Cook University, study skills online	http://www.jcu.edu.au/
American Library Association	http://www.ala.org
Curtin University	http://lsn.curtin.edu.au
Australasian Society for Computers in Learning in Tertiary Education	http://www.ascilite.org.au
Education Queensland	http://education.qld.gov.au/
Study Guides and Strategies	http://www.studygs.net/
Department of Education, Tasmania	http://www.ltag.education.tas.gov.au/
Victorian Essential Learning Standards	http://vels.vcaa.vic.edu.au/
Australian Curriculum Studies Assocation	http://www.acsa.edu.au/
Nova Mind Software	http://www.nova-mind.com/

Mind Mapping Freeware

The following freeware Mind Mapping applications may be a good place to start if you are still unsure whether Mind Mapping is for you.

You should note that freeware will, necessarily, have less functionality than the kinds of software that have been outlined in this book.

If you feel that the functionality of these tools is below that which you will need, most paid softwares offer a 30 day trial version of their software for download – this will give you a better idea as to whether a fully functional, paid software or a less functional, free software is better for your needs.

Please note that the author of this book provides the following links only for your own information, he in no way endorses these or any other free Mind Mapping software programs and takes no responsibility for their functionality or for any issues you may have with them. Further, none of these freeware providers have in any way made payment to the author to appear in this book. This list is provided for the readers information and the reader takes all responsibility when choosing to download any of these programs.

The following reviews are provided by Wikipedia (www.wikipedia.org):

http://cmap.ihmc.us/

IHMC CmapTools is a freeware web based mind mapping application. It allows for online collaboration within the mind maps.

http://bubbl.us/

bubbl.us is a free web based brainstorming application. Allows collaboration and posting mind maps to the web.

http://www.gliffy.com/

Gliffy is a freeware web based mind mapping and drawing application.

http://compendium.open.ac.uk/openlearn/index.html

Compendium is a free mind mapping application created by the Open University.

http://www.mindomo.com/

Mindomo is a free web-based Mind Mapping application that has a good set of features for a free program: rich text topics, rich text notes, hyperlinks, task info, topic images, various topic layouts, boundary around topics.

http://freemind.sourceforge.net/wiki/index.php/Main_Page

Freemind is a free Java Mind Mapping application which at the time of writing has not yet reached a version 1.0 release, but still seems to be quite popular.

Exclusive Book Owner's Forum and Extra Resources

As a special bonus for you, we have set up an exclusive area within the NovaMind forum where you can find extra resources, including the Mind Maps you have seen in this book for you to download. There is also an area for open discussion and sharing of information and ideas arising from this book, and feedback for inclusion in future versions of this book.

To join, please join the forum at http://www.nova-mind.com/Forum and then send an email to forum@nova-mind.com telling them your forum ID, and that you purchased the book, and you will be added to the access list so that next time you log in you will see the exclusive book forums.

Epilogue

Thank you for investing the time and effort in reading this book. I sincerely hope it has been of use in your ongoing quest to provide high quality educational opportunities to your students.

Mind Mapping has changed my life and while I obviously have a product that I think is amazing and would be of benefit to you, more importantly I want you to experience the same benefits that I have. If you get those benefits Mind Mapping by hand or using free software, then that is enough for me.

If you do choose to go on and use NovaMind as your Mind Mapping software then we're happy to welcome you to the family!

Please feel free to contact me at any time with feedback on this book, our web site or our software – we are always delighted to hear what our clients think about the products we produce and are committed to ongoing development and improvement of these products.

On a more personal note, I want to thank you for the job you do. It has often been said that teachers are some of the most under-valued and under-remunerated professionals in our society and I certainly think that we could do more to recognise the vital contribution that you make to our children and to our community.

I wish you all the best in your future educational endeavours, whether Mind Mapping is part of that future or not.

Gideon King

Owner and Founder

NovaMind Software

www.nova-mind.com